SKIP COLLEGE

LAUNCH YOUR CAREER WITHOUT DEBT, DISTRACTIONS, OR A DEGREE

Edited By
CONNOR BOYACK

LIBERTAS PRESS
SALT LAKE CITY, UT

Libertas Press
785 East 200 South, Suite 2
Lehi, UT 84043

Skip College: Launch Your Career Without Debt, Distractions, or a Degree — 1st ed.

ISBN-13 978-1-943521-38-8 (paperback)

For bulk orders, send inquiries to info@libertasutah.org.

10 9 8 7 6 5 4 3 2

CONTENTS

Other titles by the editor:

*Lessons from a Lemonade Stand: An
Unconventional Guide to Government*

*Passion-Driven Education: How to Use Your Child's
Interests to Ignite a Lifelong Love of Learning*

*Feardom: How Politicians Exploit Your Emotions
and What You Can Do to Stop Them*

The Tuttle Twins children's book series

All proceeds from the sale of this book will be donated to Praxis, a bootcamp apprenticeship program that helps ambitious young professionals get a jump start on their career without having to attend college.

"No matter what tests show, very little of what is taught in school is learned, very little of what is learned is remembered, and very little of what is remembered is used. The things we learn, remember, and use are the things we seek out or meet in the daily, serious, nonschool part of our lives."

—JOHN HOLT

INTRODUCTION

by Connor Boyack

For decades there has been an invisible conveyor belt shepherding young students through their schooling experience. I was on it, along with all my peers, without realizing it. In high school, I was preparing for college; it was simply what you did. I never was encouraged to question that process; it was assumed to be *the* process.

In recent years the conveyor belt has been made more visible and has even been given a name by its advocates: "college and career readiness." The purpose of college is, we're told, to help you "get a job," and high school and preceding years of schooling are all about getting you ready for that end goal. There was also that perpetual, subtle threat implied in every push to go to college: those without a college degree won't find a good job, and therefore won't succeed in life nearly as well as their degree-laden peers.

But that's changing. A recent survey of 600 human resource leaders—those responsible for hiring people for their companies, large and small—found that "90 percent were open to hiring a candidate without a four-year degree."[1] That's a staggering statistic and one that undermines the long-held notion that going to college is a prerequisite to getting a good job. As one HR manager said, "Our education system is not keeping up with the needs businesses have, and what is most important today should be proof of skills and the ability to deliver results."[2]

The accounting firm Ernst & Young is one company to ditch the degree requirement—a step they took after performing their own internal review of over 400 graduates. "It found no evidence to conclude that previous success in higher education correlated with future success in subsequent professional qualifications undertaken," observed one of the company's executives.[3] Computer giant IBM made the same decision, resulting in around 15 percent of its new hires being without a degree.[4] The company's CEO wrote in an op-ed that "jobs are being created that demand new skills—which in turn requires new approaches to education, training and recruiting."[5] Apple, Starbucks, Costco, Bank of America, and many more corporations agree and routinely hire applicants who lack a degree. Same for Google, who's HR manager said, "When you look at people who don't go to school and make their way in the world, those are exceptional human beings. And we should do everything we can to find those people."[6]

It's disturbing to watch so many people sacrifice to obtain a goal for reasons that have been proven to be inaccurate and ineffectual. The above-mentioned survey of HR leaders found that 47% felt colleges are not preparing students for the working world. And yet the conveyor belt steadily moves in the same direction, with hordes of humans being herded through college. The desire for a degree is so strong that some commit fraud to obtain it. In early 2019, international news erupted with indignation over celebrities and wealthy business magnates who had been caught in a massive cheating and bribery scandal, using their wealth and privilege to get their children admitted to college.

The lead story was that of Lori Loughlin, the famed Aunt Becky in the 90s-era sitcom Full House. Her 19-year-old daughter Olivia had reportedly begged her parents to let her focus on her social media career, but they pushed her to go to college instead. Loughlin was so desirous that her two daughters obtain degrees that she and her husband allegedly paid a $500,000 bribe to get them into school. Dozens of other parents were caught up in the indictment, with prosecutors pointing to children falsely designated as athletic recruits, proctors bribed to edit answers on standardized college-entry exams, and impersonators paid to take tests to raise students' grade-point average.[7]

Olivia was making significant money with sponsored social media posts, already neck-deep in a thriving business building her personal brand. "This is her passion," a family friend observed. "She never really understood why she needs to go to school. It was always clear that it was the parents that pushed them to go to school."[8] Indeed, Olivia herself told fans that she was going to college for "the experience of, like, game days and partying" and that "I don't really care about school, as you guys all know."[9] While plenty of comments might be made about the lack of educational depth the social media star and young woman born into wealth has revealed about herself, her story cuts to the heart of the matter: if college is ultimately about getting a good job, as its primary proponents say, then why should somebody who is already successful bother to go?

My story differs from Olivia's and tracks closely with what is probably the typical situation for high school students. I never even considered that college wasn't an option; it was presumed that it was the next logical step to take after being subjected to a decade and a half of institutional schooling. The question was not whether

I should go to college, but which ones I should apply to. My parents, like most other parents, wanted their son to be successful in life—and they, like most, had simply accepted the idea that the prerequisite for professional success was a college degree.

And so I applied—and I went. I sat through four more years of school and was taught all sorts of things I no longer remember. Even worse, I paid for the privilege! Sure, there were game days and partying, but my four years in college were an educational rite of passage that saw me memorizing and regurgitating information that had nothing to do with my field of interest. I wanted to become a web developer, creating websites and coding fun projects, yet I was forced to study philosophy, biology, trigonometry, history, and more. The problem with this approach, as I document in more detail in my book *Passion-Driven Education*, is that it was all pump-and-dump. I learned the material for the sake of getting a good grade, only to quickly forget it soon afterward because it lacked personal and professional relevance. I was jumping through (expensive) hoops to do what was required of me so I could be granted a piece of paper at the end of the experience that certified I was a good hoop-jumper.

I recall one experience with a friend who was on the verge of graduation. Despite several years of college, he didn't know what career he wanted to work towards. At the last minute, he changed majors, setting himself up for two more years of schooling. He then did it again—spending a total of nearly eight years, and a substantial amount of money, simply trying to figure out what he wanted to do with his life. It seemed to me to be a profound waste of time and resources.

It wasn't until years later that I began to really question the purpose of college. I had reached a point in my life where I considered my time scarce and valuable. And with this newfound sense of scarcity, I began to wonder why I hadn't felt it earlier. What milestones in life could I have achieved had I not spent four more years at a school desk? What career advancements might I have reached if I had a head start? These and more questions became all the more tantalizing as I began seeing more and more stories about successful college dropouts and entrepreneurs who never attended at all.

I do not believe that college is inherently problematic. There is value—educational, social, and professional—to being on a campus and obtaining a degree. And, to be sure, there are certain professions that absolutely require that you obtain a college credential. But the overall benefits of attending college have to be weighed against their alternatives. And that's precisely why the college industrial complex has exploited the conveyor belt mentality for so long, thriving on the assumption that parents inculcate into their children—that college is generally a necessary step toward a successful life. They don't want the alternatives to be considered; they prefer you not even know they exist. That's disastrous, and it's this precise ignorance that has contributed to a $1.5 trillion college debt bubble with millions of borrowers completely defaulting on their school loans.[10] As with any sizable investment—of both time and money—those interested in college should be fully informed before making a decision. Merely considering the option of not going to college is a radical first step.

The point of this book is to throw up a number of signs and detours along the conveyor belt and to help you recognize that there are alternatives to college that allow young adults to achieve personal and professional success in similar, or superior, fashion. For some careers, there is simply no option but to attend college and chase even more advanced degrees. But for the rest of us, every day presents more campus-free opportunities to launch a career without debt, distractions, or degrees.

Ready to begin?

NOTES

1. "Closing the Skills Gap," LearningHouse, accessed May 5, 2019, https://www.learninghouse.com/ closing-skills-gap-report/#section-four.

2. "Employers Open To Ditching Degree Requirements When Hiring ," *Forbes*, August 14, 2018, https://www. forbes.com/sites/gradsoflife/2018/08/14/employers-open-to-ditching-degree-requirements-when-hiring/.

3. "Ernst & Young Removes University Degree Classification From Entry Criteria As There's 'No Evidence' It Equals Success," *Huffington Post*, April 8, 2015, https://www.huffingtonpost.co.uk/2016/01/07/ ernst-and-young-removes-degree-classification-entry-criteria_n_7932590.html.

4. "Why IBM Wants to Hire Employees Who Don't Have a 4-year College Degree," CNBC, November 7, 2017, https://www.cnbc.com/2017/11/07/why-ibm-wants-to-hire-employees-who-dont-have-a-4-year-college-degree.html.

5. "We Need to Fill 'New Collar' Jobs that Employers Demand: IBM's Rometty," USA Today, December 13, 2016, https://www.usatoday.com/story/tech/colum-nist/2016/12/13/we-need-fill-new-collar-jobs-employ-ers-demand-ibms-rometty/95382248/.

6. "15 More Companies That No Longer Require a Degree—Apply Now," Glassdoor, August 14, 2018, https://www.glassdoor.com/blog/no-degree-required/.

7. "Actresses, Business Leaders and Other Wealthy Parents Charged in U.S. College Entry Fraud," *The New York Times*, March 12, 2019, https://www.nytimes. com/2019/03/12/us/college-admissions-cheating-scandal.html.

8. "Lori Loughlin and Her Husband Are 'Finding Out Who Their Real Friends Are' Amid Scandal: Source," *People*, March 14, 2019, https://people.com/tv/

college-admissions-scandal-lori-loughlin-mossimo-giannulli-friends/.

9.   "Lori Loughlin's Daughter Olivia Said She Didn't 'Really Care About School' Before Heading to College," Entertainment Tonight, March 12, 2019, https://www.yahoo.com/entertainment/lori-loughlin-apos-daughter-olivia-180934432.html.

10. "The New Toll of American Student Debt in 3 Charts," *The New York Times*, July 11, 2018, https://www.nytimes.com/2018/07/11/your-money/student-loan-debt-parents.html.

"The aim of public education is not to spread enlightenment at all, it is simply to reduce as many individuals as possible to the same safe level, to breed and train a standardized citizenry, to put down dissent and originality."[1]

H.L. Mencken

HOW WE GOT HERE

THE CONVEYOR BELT OF MODERN SCHOOLING

by John Taylor Gatto

The road, or conveyor belt, that carried the human race from education (as the one-of-a-kind process of developing independence for individuals) to being "schooled" (like fish) was a very strange one. So, as I walk you through it, try to visualize each step. That will make its weirdness easier to remember and, eventually, to escape.

American education, from the beginnings of our nation as a colony of Great Britain, was aimed at producing *competencies*—awareness and knowledge—to make us self-sufficient, but that practical aim of edu-

---

John Taylor Gatto was a 30-year, award-winning public school teacher. A popular speaker and author of multiple books on education reform, John wrote this chapter as his last piece of content before he passed away on October 25, 2018.

cation changed radically in the mid-19th century, at the hands of an ambitious Massachusetts socialist politician, to being a *psychological conditioning laboratory* aimed at producing obedience to orders from superiors in rank, social class, and wealth.

The story of our schools begins in 1806, in the military dictatorship of Prussia, in Germany, during the Napoleonic wars. Napoleon Bonaparte, a military genius, was the true energy source which caused your neighborhood schools to occur in the following fashion.

Napoleon conquered Prussia in the battle of Jena in 1806 with his non-professional soldiers. French occupiers took over Berlin, humiliating the proud Prussians, whose army had been considered the most dominant in the world. Panic descended on Prussia, whose intellectual leaders decided that disobedience among enlisted soldiers and disobeying officers had caused their defeat.

The head of philosophy at the University of Berlin, Johann Fichte, wrote a series of essays to the Prussian King, Frederick William III, demanding that children (who later would be soldiers) be raised by the political state in forced-obedience institutions, called "schools," to learn absolute obedience to orders under the pretext that it was "education."

Fichte's *Addresses to the German Nation* demanded that imagination in the young be destroyed as the root cause of political resistance.

Fichte's book was, and is, widely available in America, whose population was, and is, over 50% German in ancestry; and in 1843, a German-ancestry American politician Horace Mann, head of the Boston School Committee, wrote a document simply known to history as "The Letter" to his committee, urging that Prussian schooling be imposed by legal compulsion on the children of Massachusetts. In 1852 it was done, and then it was copied in New York State one year later, and from there, by the inducement of personal government "pay-offs," the system spread state by state, from coast to coast across America.

Notable characteristics of Prussian compulsion schools are these:

1. Learning and scholarship skills are irrelevant, obedience is the priority; enthusiastic obedience to government orders is mandatory
2. Personal wishes are of no consequence
3. Original, independent thinking, is discouraged
4. Relationships with peers are made difficult
5. Nobody without a state license can "teach"
6. Memorized "facts" are the substances tested, not skills

7. Passive confinement to chairs is the daily reality for 12 years
8. No raw experience is offered
9. No educators are permitted with which to learn personal strengths and limitations
10. No explorations are permitted without official authorization
11. The "curriculum" to be learned is standardized, the same for all; Testing, too, is standardized
12. Contact with outside schoolrooms is strictly limited

In the long history of the human race, until the mid-19th century, no such institution as universal forced schooling (following a government design) ever occurred, because the idea is so ridiculous on its face. No nation or people would ever accept the notion, although utopian, fanciful thinkers sometimes proposed it. Great empires rose in Egypt, Greece, Rome, and Asia—all without formalized indoctrination and training—and it was made possible through a process of emulation: new generations imitated previous generations and improved upon their methods; sons imitated fathers; priests and military heroes arranged goals for the community—arrived at by individualized routes and not centralized dogma. The problems of specific areas dictated what was studied and learned at any given time, through imitation of those already competent in those subjects, trades, and skills.

Consider America's settlement as a British colony. Between the 16th century and the late 18th century, the revolutionary nation of the United States became one of the strongest nations on earth—relatively wealthy, powerful and "civilized"—without any formal schooling at government hands.

How could that sort of expansive growth and prosperity possibly happen without any of Fichte's schools in America producing obedient citizens, when every family was providing a tailor-made education to their own children, in a private, customized, flexible and personal way?

Germany is the key to understand how American Education mutated into American Schooling—the result of which has led to a drastic decline in our growth and prosperity, having forsaken education for a system of making students think alike.

"School" was first realized in Prussia, Germany, borne from a militarized, intolerant and socialistic society where personal behavior was so tightly controlled that women had to register their periods (start and finish) with the police, where free speech and associations were not civil rights, and where social class origins dictated (to a great extent) your occupation for life. What sort of system of education would produce such fierce and subservient minds on demand?

School in Prussia existed to create obedient soldiers, not to educate independent, self-reliant citizens. Prussia was internationally accepted as the finest army on earth; Prussian soldiers marched into battle twirling their rifles and bayonets to impress the enemy!

Another huge boost to Prussian schooling in America was its universal promotion by American colleges, which occurred in a peculiar way. Prussia was the only place on earth where a PhD was issued, as they invented them. As a result of the instant social status of said degree, thousands of Americans from influential families traveled there from 1800-1830, to obtain that fashionable distinction, known as a "doctorate" degree. When the freshly minted PhDs returned to America, they became the presidents of almost all major American universities and spread Prussian thinking to every state in the country.

To fully understand Prussian thinking and values, two famously influential European philosophers, Benedict Spinoza of Holland, and Thomas Hobbes of England (both favorites of Thomas Jefferson) must be read. Hobbes' *Leviathan*, published in 1651, promoted the idea that a strong, centralized government—what we would today call "fascist"—was necessary before civilization could occur, because human nature was so murderous and selfish that people couldn't live in peace together without government regulating lives closely. Spinoza, about 19 years later, published his *Tractatus Theologico-Politicus*, in 1670, which reinterpreted the Bible to be a document intended to teach obedience and taught national leaders that as long as faith-based religions provided moral teaching to the young, no nation could be loyal to kings and secular leaders. What had to replace faith-based religions, to bring stability and peace to society, was a "secular religion" in the form of schools that taught the kind of morality elites wished to be taught. After reading Spinoza's *Tractatus*, Jefferson proposed a system of universal, government-run, secular schools to teach whatever principles the government wanted people to believe.

Prussia accepted Hobbes' and Spinoza's concepts of the "best society," through a third philosopher, a German idealist, Georg Hegel, and thereby ordained forced schooling based on an elite design, by law, for the first time in human history.

America, influenced by Jefferson's views of Hobbes and Spinoza, as well as the evangelism for Prussian schooling ushered in by Horace Mann, used federal money to spread Prussian schooling into every state between 1852 (Massachusetts) and 1918 (Mississippi).

In Prussian schooling, only the government's "master" curriculum counts—what individuals want is irrelevant—and the knowledge that matters (to the government) is sanitized and standardized; whereby it can only be administered and delivered by employees licensed by the political state. It was this formulation of a centralized, universal, state-controlled school system that, in part, led to the downfall of Germany and the rise of the National Socialist, or Nazi, party.

Germany entered American schooling in significant fashion after 1933, when Adolf Hitler expelled a group of Marxist intellectuals from Frankfurt, Germany. In 1933 they came to New York through Columbia University, with its "teachers' college," and to California, by way of Hollywood. This group and their intellectual philosophy are known to history as "The Frankfurt School."

These men, deadly afraid of capitalism and American culture, enthusiastically conceived of a new way to undermine and destroy capitalism. By 1917 Marxism had destroyed the Russian Empire, by way of economic communism, pitting working-class individuals violently against middle and upper-class ones. But the Frankfurt thinkers, led by Vladimir Lenin, head of the communist Soviet Union, said the strength of capitalism is in its cultural institutions, its schools, churches, architecture, films, family relations, sexual habits, gender, media, and in the arts in general—music, painting, fashion, holidays, etc. The new revolutionary strategy would be to infiltrate the culture and weaken it until the common citizens were demoralized.

In schooling, this was done by profoundly weakening the intellectual curriculum, setting goals to abandoning dialectical (critical comparison) thinking, studies of classic literature, and linguistic fluency; degrading the teaching of history; and omitting economics and philosophy entirely. Instead, the objective was to fill students' heads with official propaganda and "spin," resulting in the standardizing of students— making them cogs in a machine which they could never see, feel, or understand. This is the opposite of what education should be and is demonstrative of a system of controlling minds, generation after generation.

SCHOOLING TODAY

In America, in the 21st century, we force public school children to pass through a system designed in the 19th century, for the purpose of creating obedient soldiers. Is there any doubt that that is less than appropriate for a nation committed to free will, personal sovereignty, individual independence, high-tech imagination, and negotiation in place of warfare?

Until the implementation and reliance upon Prussian forced schooling are abandoned in our schools, our children will never have a real education.

We have little hope of supplying our young with an appropriate education to fit their circumstances and to help them learn how to survive and thrive in life, given the school system as it currently exists. To wish that it will evolve and change to benefit students is naïve, considering the source and historical evolution of schooling.

THE FUTURE OF FREEDOM

What is the solution to this system of schooling which we have inherited?

I think you're doing it right now.

You're reading; you're thinking; you're growing in the right direction. No instructor or teacher is forcing you to read this; you're doing it because you want to.

You are pursuing your interests; you are outgrowing the status quo. You are seeking cognitive liberty; you are attaining it through action.

You can't change the world with just a wish, but you can inspire others to do likewise through your informed actions. The best teaching is not in schools—it's by your example.

Freedom is learned, not inherited; it is the result of acquiring a skill set which includes intellectual self-defense, physical self-defense, and non-aggression. These are the ingredients of freedom, and the loss of any single ingredient leads to the downfall of both the individual and the group.

The best education is one pursued by each human being, one mind at a time, by choosing to follow one's interests; not by subscribing to a system which programs minds as they travel down the conveyor belt toward a reality they are ill-prepared to face.

It's time we learned some of these essential lessons. As we do, children, families, and all people will prosper—now, and for generations to come.

NOTES

1. H.L. Mencken, "The Little Red Schoolhouse," *The American Mercury, vol. 1*, (New York: Alfred Knoff, 1924) 504.

"It is perfectly possible for a man to be out of prison and yet not free—to be under no physical constraint and yet to be a psychological captive, compelled to think, feel and act as the representatives of the national State, or of some private interest within the nation, want him to think, feel and act."[1]

Aldous Huxley

INDOCTRINATION FACTORIES

OPEN MINDS ARE CLOSING ON CAMPUS

by Brittany Hunter

College used to hold a sacred place in Western culture. On the cusp of adulthood, young people left the security of their families for the first time and set out to become their own unique and individual beings. Once under the guidance of their professors and mentors, these young students were exposed to new ideas and theories that were to be deliberated down to their finest points until each student arrived at their own conclusions. In the pursuit of knowledge, keeping an open mind was of the utmost importance.

Brittany Hunter is a senior writer at the Foundation for Economic Education. Follow her work at FEE.org and connect with her on Twitter @Britt_the_wit.

Academia, however, no longer represents the quest to obtain knowledge and young adults are no longer encouraged to keep an open mind.

Rather than exposing students to new ideas and teaching them *how* to think about complex issues, young minds are coddled and kept isolated from any knowledge that goes against the status quo. In many regards, students today are only taught *what* to think. As a result, campuses have become a place where minds are closing.

THIS ISN'T WHAT I EXPECTED

My first day of college was filled with boundless hope. Finally old enough to live away from home and form my own worldviews, my undergrad education was supposed to expose me to a wide range of opinions and ideas to consider. Over the next four years, the knowledge I gained was going to help me become an independent thinker fully capable of approaching any situation with an open mind and able to navigate any obstacle the real world might throw at me.

This was my time to expose myself to as many new ideas as possible. Growing up in my home town, I had always felt sheltered. And even though I wasn't moving away for school, I had convinced myself that my time as an undergrad would help me become more cultured and well-rounded.

In the days leading up to the start of the semester, I conjured up images of how lectures might unfold. I imagined a professor with elbow patches on his worn sports coat, pacing back and forth, not just lecturing, but creating an open dialogue with his students, questioning them like Socrates.

After years of being treated like a child in the public school system, college was going to be my first mature and sophisticated educational experience. This time around, the only students present in class would be the ones who had paid to be there, rather than those mandated by law to attend. And the professors were not merely teachers, but academics—true intellectuals with a wealth of knowledge to bestow upon me.

That's what I thought would happen, anyway.

My first class was U.S. history, and within the first few minutes of my professor's introduction, she had found a way to voice her support for the newly elected President Obama. She also found a way to squeeze in a passionate monologue describing how little she thought of the Americans who had chosen to vote for another candidate. It seemed odd to have brought up the recent election at all since our class only covered the 18th century. But 2008 had been a historic election and, while I had not supported either of the mainstream candidates, the enthusiasm over Barack Obama's win was understandably exciting. So I dismissed this endorsement as a symptom of the era of "hope and change" and didn't think of it again for the remainder of the class period.

My second class was Introductory Psychology. After briefly introducing the syllabus for the semester, my professor switched topics entirely and asked each student to go around the room disclosing our political affiliations. When a student would identify as "conservative" or "Republican," a look of disgust and disappointment came over her face. She had broken the room into three parts and after we had responded, we were each sent to join our fellow Republicans, Democrats, or Independents in different corners of the room. This created an awkward political divide among my classmates, one nobody would have been aware of had the professor not gone out of her way to draw lines in the sand.

From time to time throughout the semester, that same professor would throw out facts to the class with her political spin attached at the end. "The birth control pill is 99.9 percent effective," she said once. She then quickly followed up with, "And Republicans have done everything in their power to deny women the right to birth control over the years."

Not only were these comments completely untrue and irrelevant to introductory psych, but since we now had at least a vague idea of which of our classmates identified as Republican, her comments also served to grow the divide. Those being passive-aggressively called out now felt compelled to stay quiet in class, while those who agreed with the professor felt a sort of militant duty to take on the conservative students and challenge their opinions during class discussions.

As a political science major, I had expected to participate in routine political debates during my undergrad years. However, I had naively assumed that these arguments would be confined to my political science courses, rather than facing them at every turn.

That is not to say that my political science courses themselves were not especially challenging. Within the first few weeks of the semester, my political ideologies professor asked the students to take a position on gun control and then use compelling arguments to defend that position in an essay. Choosing to defend the position that the right to bear arms is sacred and guaranteed to each individual by the U.S. Constitution, I pored myself into my work constructing a paper that logically laid out my thoughts. When the paper was handed back to me, it bore a bold, red "C." While the paper itself had been well executed, the professor had declared that I had chosen the wrong side of the debate and docked my grade accordingly.

So far, this was not how I had imagined college, and it all got worse from there. During my first political internship, I had to send an email to my French professor, asking to miss class in order to volunteer on election day. The response I received said, "Of course you can take that time off, so long as your candidate is not a Republican." While the response was followed by a smiley face emoji, the comment itself did not seem appropriate for a professor to make to a student.

Instances like this kept occurring, and college was already beginning to lose its luster. After the aforementioned psychology professor had hired me to work part-time as her teaching assistant, she asked me how I felt about nationalized healthcare during a casual conversation in her office. I responded that I did not think the government had a role in something that was so clearly a market issue. My professor was silent.

A week later I was called into her office and told that our professional relationship was not working out, and she was going to have to relieve me of my duties. It appeared that when I sorted myself as an "independent" that first day in class, she assumed I leaned far-left on the political spectrum. To be fair, she had only offered three options, none of which described me, so I chose as best I could. However, when my true leanings were revealed, she no longer saw a reason to associate with me.

I thought I had come to college for healthy civil discourse on some of the most controversial subjects facing our modern world. Instead, a very clear political and social agenda seemed to be pushed on the students in just about every corner of my campus. The administration and the majority of the faculty members didn't seem to have any use for deliberation and debate; they just wanted to tell us what we should believe. And, unfortunately, many of my fellow classmates were all too eager to adopt whatever opinions were presented to them as fact.

Once most of the students had bought into whatever worldview was being pushed on them by their instructors, they became missionaries for the cause, eager to start an argument in class or "correct" someone who disagreed with their newly adopted framework. However, none of the arguments being made paid much attention to reason. Instead, I found myself frequently engaged in contentious discussions with classmates and professors all keen on using emotional pleas in place of rational arguments.

On the eve of my freshman midterm examinations, I had a stark realization: my campus was not the haven of free thought I had previously believed it to be. This was not the place to question authority or challenge the status quo. This was a machine, and each semester it pumped out carbon copies of graduates all taught to regurgitate the same talking points and hold the same beliefs. And anyone—student or professor alike—who offered a dissenting opinion ran the risk of being targeted for retaliation by the campus administration.

But the political and social biases that were plaguing my campus were not exclusive to my school alone. As the years dragged on, campuses across the country became increasingly vigilant in silencing those who went against the approved rhetoric.

NOT JUST MY CAMPUS

In 2015, Devorah Goldman of the *Weekly Standard* wrote a shocking article about the political biases she witnessed while she was working on her graduate degree at Hunter College.[2]

After being asked to stay after class one day, Goldman was informed that her political views were making the professor and the other students uncomfortable. She was even warned that students with "conservative" opinions had encountered problems graduating from Hunter in the past. Her professor then asked Goldman to stop participating in class discussions. She wrote:

> I spent the rest of that semester mostly quiet, frustrated, and missing my undergraduate days, when my professors encouraged intellectual diversity and give-and-take. I attempted to take my case to a higher-up at school, an extremely nice, fair professor who insisted that it was in my own best interest not to rock the boat.[3]

She later continued:

> It was laughable in its own way, though. My school was ostensibly all about freedom of expression. In our mandatory 5-hour diversity awareness training, we were each asked what pronouns we prefer to use when describing ourselves. We could dress and identify sexually virtually any way we wanted, though some fashion choices and sexual identities were more celebrated than others. We talked about how to approach clients whose gender identities were difficult to pinpoint. There was a special gender-neutral bathroom on the fourth floor that seemed rarely used. We were allowed to differ; we could not disagree.[4]

Like my own campus, Hunter had begun shutting out any opposing thought. Anyone who offered a contradictory opinion was on the wrong side of the argument. Of her own experience, Goldman concluded:

> Sadly, my teachers all seemed to take their cues from the same playbook; they were very nice people with frightening messages. In my teacher's mind, two adults could not hold two different opinions. Any dissent was simply due to a lack of comprehension on one or both of their parts.

In addition to being targeted inside the classroom, student activists across the country have also faced retaliation over their club affiliations. The college group Young Americans for Liberty routinely sponsors Know Your Rights campaigns, where members hand out pocket-sized versions of the United States Constitution to other students. Unfortunately, this has resulted in several members being confronted and arrested by campus police officers who claim these students are violating school policy.

I witnessed similar occurrences on my own campus, specifically with right-leaning political groups. However, the Revolutionary Student Union (AKA the "Marxists") was never reprimanded or stopped from walking around campus holding signs that read "death to capitalists." It's odd that the Constitution is considered offensive while violent statements are viewed as acceptable.

All public colleges and universities that receive federal funding are bound to honor and protect constitutional rights, including the First Amendment right to free speech. However, many colleges are able to get around this obligation thanks to "free speech zones."

While instituted much earlier, free speech zones became more prominent on college campuses in the early 2000s. The ever-expanding war on terror had sparked a resurgence of the anti-war movement, which subsequently resulted in a rise of campus demonstrations and protests. In order to contain the chaos and protect any prominent pro-war or pro-Bush speakers, many colleges were compelled to confine free speech to tiny, fenced-off areas, placed far from the center of campus life.

This has made it all too easy for campuses to cite students for demonstrating outside of their designated free speech zone. And if the administrators don't like what is being said, students have a greater chance of becoming a target. Unfortunately, many campuses have decided that they don't want their students to know their constitutional rights. Luckily, there is at least one organization that exists primarily to protect and defend campus free speech. The entire mission of the

Foundation for Individual Rights in Education (FIRE) is to "defend and sustain the individual rights of students and faculty members at America's colleges and universities. These rights include freedom of speech, freedom of association, due process, legal equality, religious liberty, and sanctity of conscience—the essential qualities of liberty."[5]

Over the years, FIRE has been integral in providing legal resources and helping students fight back against oppressive campuses that blatantly violate each student's right to free speech and that contribute to the further closing of minds on campus. And thanks to their assistance, students have been able to successfully fight back against oppressive campus administrations.

Yet, the fact that the sanctity of free speech—and thus the free exchange of ideas—has deteriorated so much as to warrant the existence of FIRE at all shows us how far colleges have strayed from their intended purpose. No longer do institutions invite those with controversial or opposing viewpoints to campus for their students' consideration. And these days, the students themselves are all too eager to riot if confronted with something they don't understand.

THE CRADLE OF FREE SPEECH

The state of free speech on the American college campus has been getting progressively worse over the last few decades. The 2016 election season escalated the problem to new heights as the reality of a "President Trump" caused massive hysteria on the "left."

The day after Trump was declared the winner, campuses across the country announced they would be offering counseling support to students traumatized by his win. While already in the news, the spread of "safe spaces" across U.S. campuses rose as students seemed almost incapable of controlling their emotions. All this would soon come to a head when the University of California, Berkeley became ground zero in the fight to secure the future of free speech on campus.

Often referred to as the "cradle of free speech," Berkeley was the site that gave birth to the Free Speech Movement that began in 1964. On a cold December evening, graduate student Mario Savio led 1,000 of his fellow students in a peaceful protest against the campus administration. In front of Sproul Hall, the students conducted a sit-in and demanded that the administration stop restricting political activity on campus. As the protest continued on into the night, school president Clark Kerr grew restless and demanded everyone leave. When the crowd remained, Kerr decried the demonstration as "an instrument of anarchy." That was when the police were let loose on the crowd.

By the end of the night, nearly 800 students had been arrested. *The Washington Post* recalls:

> "'An Army of law officers broke up a massive sit-in occupation,' reported the Associated Press, which described 'limply defiant' protesters being dragged down the stairs on their backs and shoved into police vans. 'Cries of police brutality rose from demonstration supporters watching outside.'[6]

In his now famous address, "The Machine Speech" protest organizer Savio lambasted the campus administration's attempts to violate First Amendment rights:

> There's a time when the operation of the machine becomes so odious, makes you so sick at heart that you can't take part! You can't even passively take part! And you've got to put your bodies upon the gears and upon the wheels, upon the levers, upon all the apparatus—and you've got to make it stop! And you've got to indicate to the people who run it, to the people who own it—that unless you're free the machine will be prevented from working at all!! [7]

This passion and unwavering dedication to free speech and expression used to define Berkeley's student body, but not anymore.

In February 2017, avid Trump supporter and political provocateur Milo Yiannopoulos was invited to give an address to Berkeley students. Yiannopoulos had risen to popularity during the 2016 election season after building his entire public persona on making shocking political and social commentary. It was no surprise, then, that his invitation to speak at Berkeley sparked outrage on campus. It also didn't take long for the student body to begin circulating a petition demanding that the administration cancel the event.

Over 1,500 people gathered in front of Sproul Hall to protest Yiannopoulos' appearance—the very place where Savio passionately stood up for the right to free speech so many years prior. As a college that received public tax dollars, Berkeley is bound to protect the constitutional right to free speech, even when it does not agree with the speaker in question.

For the most part, the protestors had remained peaceful. However, when a violent minority of Antifa and Black Bloc agitators began their trail of destruction, the situation escalated quickly. Fires were set, property was destroyed, and fireworks were ignited—terrifying the crowd. To make matters worse, these violent individuals were also attacking other protestors with whom they were in agreement. It was sheer madness.

Ultimately, the event was canceled because the police could not ensure the security of the building. But this was just the start of Berkeley's betrayal of free expression.

In April of that year, Ann Coulter was scheduled to speak on campus and was met with similar violence and hostility. The university once again canceled the event, this time on the grounds of speaker safety. However, as criticism began to circulate, Berkeley officials did offer to reschedule Coulter's appearance, an offer she declined. Coulter asserted that the school had tried to place restrictions on her right to free speech. The student group hosting her, Young America's Foundation, even threatened to sue the school.

Even outspoken progressive late-night host Bill Maher was outraged over what had happened. He told CNN's S. E. Cupp, "Berkeley, you know, used to be the cradle of free speech. And now it's just the cradle for f---ing babies."[8]

Throughout 2017, smaller right-leaning rallies and public speakers would be met with hordes of students eager to protest. And Berkeley wasn't alone. All over the nation, students were protesting and refusing to let opposing sides voice their opinions. It was almost as though they were scared of hearing what these speakers had to say.

What is ultimately so disturbing about these protests is how quickly the students resorted to violence. Why couldn't they just let these speakers come and speak their mind? The unwillingness to listen reeked of emotional immaturity. It was like watching toddlers, red in the face with index fingers lodged in their ears, stubbornly refusing to listen to their parents.

If these students were so sure that their beliefs were correct, they might consider inviting a different speaker to counter the points being made by Yiannopoulos or Coulter. If they were so outraged at the other side for vocalizing their opinions, why not encourage all sides to do the same so that everyone has a pulpit from which to preach? Perhaps a large part of the problem was that the administration and many of the professors encouraged this behavior.

THE INTELLECTUAL DARK WEB

While the students might be more prone to violence, campus administrators and overzealous professors have played a large role in perpetuating the closing of the collegiate mind. Professors have an important duty to act as stewards and mentors to young minds, leading them to form their own conclusions, but never forcing any construct upon anyone. But instead of heeding the call and rising to the occasion, many academics have chosen instead to adopt the role of propagandist with their students.

Rather than encouraging students to hear what the other side has to say, the academic elite has adopted the attitude that all those who disagree with their opinions are immoral, racist, and intolerant. Faculty and campus administrations have even targeted colleagues who hold views contrary to their own.

Anyone—professor or student—who fails to conform to the academically approved norms has a target on their backs. Where once college represented a secure space for the free exchange and deliberation of new ideas, it is now no longer so. By speaking your mind and sharing your opinions, you now run the risk of being ridiculed and proverbially burned at the stake for your beliefs.

In universities today, many professors are afraid to perform the duties of their job and actually expose students to new ideas, lest they be blacklisted and shunned from the rest of the academic world. Students, on the other hand, fear the implications that disagreeing with a professor might have on their grade. They also worry that offering differing opinions during lectures might cost them social capital with classmates. These witch hunts now define campus culture around the country as everyone seems eager to "out" and destroy the reputations of anyone holding opinions that deviate from the designated norm.

And in the absence of open and civil discourse, no real education can be obtained. Students are merely conditioned to say certain things in order to elicit a positive response from their professor, and then condemn all others who disagree. But there are still those who have a thirst for knowledge. And those diligently seeking truth and knowledge will eventually find it.

With it no longer safe to share opinions or express dissent on campus, many were forced to bring their opinions underground, sparking the birth of what would later be called the Intellectual Dark Web (IDW). While not all members come from the academic world, the rise of the IDW came as a response to what was happening on colleges campuses across North America.

For most of human history, information and knowledge have been reserved only for those who could afford to pay for the privilege. But the digital world has decentralized knowledge and, thus, made education and truth-seeking accessible to anyone with an Internet connection. Modern-day philosophers don't need a classroom in order to teach so long as they can record a podcast or upload a video to YouTube. And with college leaving so many students hungry for a real education, there is a growing market for alternative sources of knowledge.

Last spring, *New York Times* journalist Bari Weiss wrote "Meet the Renegades of the Intellectual Dark Web," in which she attempted to define the IDW. She wrote:

> Most simply, it is a collection of iconoclastic thinkers, academic renegades and media personalities who are having a rolling conversation—on podcasts, YouTube and Twitter, and in sold-out auditoriums—that sound unlike anything else happening, at least publicly, in the culture right now. Feeling largely locked out of legacy outlets, they are rapidly building their own mass media channels.[9]

Weiss continued:

> Here are some things that you will hear when you sit down to dinner with the vanguard of the Intellectual Dark Web: There are fundamental biological differences between men and women. Free speech is under siege. Identity politics is a toxic ideology that is tearing American society apart. And we're in a dangerous place if these ideas are considered 'dark.'[10]

While each member of the IDW hails from a different background, they each have the same aim: encouraging individuals to have civil conversations about their different beliefs. In a time when everything is so polarized, the IDW is proving itself to be just what our society needs. IDW member Joe Rogan commented, "People are starved for controversial opinions and they are starved for an actual conversation."[11]

In addition to Joe Rogan, some other members of the IDW include Sam Harris, Maajid Nawaz, Dave Rubin, Claire Lehmann, Ben Shapiro, Douglas Murray, Jonathan Haidt, and Christina Hoff Sommers. And the list goes on. Each of these members is challenging the status quo by offering perspectives no longer acceptable in mainstream culture.

Christina Hoff Sommers, for example, has challenged what it means to be a feminist in the modern era by calling out many third- and fourth-wave feminists. Sommers has famously said:

> I call [fourth-wave feminism] fainting–couch feminism, a la the delicate Victorian ladies who retreated to an elegant chaise when overcome with emotion. As an equality feminist from the 1970s, I am dismayed by this new craze. Women are not children. We are not fragile little birds who can't cope with jokes, works of art, or controversial speakers. Trigger warnings and

safe spaces are an infantilizing setback for feminism—and for women.[12]

But this isn't just a club for the rich and politically famous. Many of the members of the IDW are disenfranchised academics who are using alternative forms of media to reach their audiences.

It wasn't so long ago that Bret Weinstein was a respected and tenured biology professor at Evergreen State College. A Bernie Sanders supporter who is sympathetic to the sentiments of the Occupy Wall Street movement, Weinstein seems like he would fit right in on the Olympia, Washington campus.

However, in 2017 Weinstein was thrust into the public spotlight when he spoke out against his campus' participation in the Day of Absence. On this designated day, minority students are encouraged to stay home. Traditionally, the Day of Absence was to show students how colorless and dull their campuses would be without diversity. But in 2017, a group of students proposed that this year the Day of Absence should be reversed and every white student should stay home.

The proposal asked that white students refrain from coming to campus for an entire day and that they should instead go out into their communities and start conversations about race and diversity. This did not bode well for many, Weinstein included. Weinstein questioned the motives of this event and refused to participate. He even wrote a now-infamous email in which he said:

> There is a huge difference between a group or coalition deciding to voluntarily absent themselves from a shared space in order to highlight their vital and underappreciated roles (the theme of the Douglas Turner Ward play Day of Absence, as well as the recent Women's Day walkout), and a group encouraging another group to go away... The first is a forceful call to consciousness, which is, of course, crippling to the logic of oppression. The second is a show of force, and an act of oppression in and of itself.[13]

It didn't take long before students began demanding that Weinstein be fired from the school. Protests ensued and there are even YouTube videos of students confronting Weinstein and calling him a racist. Both Weinstein and his wife, Heather Heying, were long-time professors at Evergreen. But after the controversy, both resigned from their posts. Weinstein ended up filing a lawsuit on the grounds that the school had failed to protect him from "hostility based on race," asserting that the school had

> permitted, cultivated, and perpetuated a racially hostile and retaliatory work environment...

Through a series of decisions made at the highest levels, including to officially support a day of racial segregation, the college has refused to protect its employees from repeated provocative and corrosive verbal and written hostility based on race, as well as threats of physical violence.[14]

The school ended up settling with Weinstein for $500,000. Since leaving his post, Weinstein has become a full-time member of the IDW. Since he no longer had a teaching position, Weinstein began speaking at events and going on the podcasts and the shows of other IDW members, sharing his story to as many people as possible.

Since colleges were no longer satisfying the educational thirst of their students, the conversation had to be taken elsewhere; intellectuals like Sommers and Weinstein were bringing the conversation online.

Each of the members of the IDW has a harrowing story of being cast off by the mainstream, but there is, perhaps, no member quite as controversial as clinical psychologist and University of Toronto professor, Dr. Jordan B. Peterson.

Prior to 2016, Peterson led a relatively quiet life. But in September of that year, Peterson recorded a

YouTube video that would later make him a leading figure, if not the godfather, of the IDW.

CLEAN YOUR ROOM

In the fall of 2016, the Canadian government proposed a new law, Bill C-16, which sought to amend the Human Rights Act and mandate the use of certain gender pronouns. Worried about the future of free speech and the dangerous precedent this new law would set, Peterson began vigorously speaking out against the bill.

His videos went viral and before he knew it, the professor found himself being asked to share his views on a variety of news outlets. The more attention he was given, the louder students began to protest against him.

The University of Toronto eventually sent him two warning letters, requesting that he stop speaking out about the issue. But, instead of backing down in the face of opposition, Peterson committed himself to speak the truth. Instead of being frightened by the students calling him a bigot, he went into crowds of protesters and tried to have conversations to encourage understanding—but to no avail. The students—and some of his colleagues—had no interest in having any sort of conversation. They just wanted to scream.

It wasn't long before Peterson was considered toxic in academic circles. Anyone who showed any support for his work was labeled a racist or a bigot and dismissed without being heard. On one Canadian campus, the administration felt so threatened by Peterson's message that they reprimanded a student for showing a video of him during class. Lindsay Shepherd was a student and TA at Wilfrid Laurier University in Waterloo, Ontario. As part of one of her lessons for a communications course, she played a video clip in which Peterson discussed his views on Bill C-16.

Not long after, Shepard was called in to have a meeting with the campus administration who chastised her for creating a "toxic environment" for her students. She was also told that showing the video without first condemning and vilifying Peterson was like "neutrally playing a speech by Hitler." Only on modern college campuses would someone dare to compare a free speech advocate to Adolf Hitler.

Shepherd was wise and, anticipating that this meeting would go as it did, secretly recorded the meeting with the administration. Afterward, she handed the recording over to the media, giving the world a firsthand look at how low campus administrations were willing to go to suppress opposing thought.

After capitulating to public pressure, Wilfrid Laurier University was forced to issue an apology to Shepherd. Shepherd took to Twitter and commented:

> Moral of the story: A university must be repeatedly publicly shamed, internationally, in order to apologize (oh, but keep the task force & investigation)...Even then, ambiguous about free speech. Also, make sure to secretly record all meetings or they won't take you seriously.[15]

This wouldn't be the end of the academics' attacks on Peterson or his followers. Since Peterson, like Ben Shapiro and other IDW members, speak often about the biological differences between men and women, they have been dismissed as sexist members of the patriarchy. Let that sink in for one moment: pointing out the biological differences between men and women is now grounds for being labeled a sexist.

Even though these claims of sexism are false, Peterson's opinions have left him open to constant criticism from other "intellectuals." Peterson, though, is no stranger to the world of academia and he is well aware of the dire situation on college campuses. He has used his platform to speak out against young adults wasting their money—or their parents' money—on college:

> If you're a taxpayer or paying for your kid's liberal arts degree, you're underwriting this gang

of nihilists. You're supporting ideologues who claim that all truth is subjective, that all sex differences are socially constructed, and that Western imperialism is the sole source of all Third World problems. They're the post-modernists pushing progressive activism at a college near you.[16]

Peterson has experienced a tidal wave of success, selling out huge arenas across the United States and Canada. He has inspired an entire generation of young adults to not only question what they are being taught, but to get their own lives in order before they attempt to control or change others.

Peterson, as well as others in the IDW, have responded to the closing of minds on campus by providing alternative sources of knowledge to young adults who are desperate for information. And since the IDW offers so many differing viewpoints, it has, in a sense, created a new marketplace of ideas—replacing the need to pay for a college education.

WHAT HAPPENED TO OPEN MINDS?

The examples given throughout this chapter are not isolated instances. Where once colleges stood for enlightenment, they now exist solely to program students and confirm preexisting biases. But why has this happened?

We have made the grave error of assuming that since colleges and universities are traditionally where the intellectuals go, there is no need to search for knowledge and truth off-campus. You wouldn't go to a library looking for a surgeon, after all. But when it comes to getting an education, nothing could be further from the truth. Too many students enter college and, instead of diligently seeking wisdom, refer only to the knowledge of their professors. Professors, however, are fallible beings like the rest of us, subject to their own biases and shortcomings.

Philosopher Karl Popper once wrote, "our ignorance is sobering and boundless," and nothing could be more true of the current campus culture. In thinking that knowledge is already earned, many people stop seeking it. And as a result, their ignorance grows.

Popper continued:

> With each step forward, with each problem which we solve, we not only discover new and unsolved problems, but we also discover that where we believed that we were standing on firm and safe ground, all things are, in truth, insecure and in a state of flux.[17]

He also later added, "There are no ultimate sources of knowledge," which might help to explain why institutions of higher education have contributed so much to the closing of minds. With knowledge now so decentralized, colleges no longer have the monopoly on education. And instead of working to innovate with the modern times, colleges have doubled down.

In Jordan Peterson's bestselling book, *12 Rules for Life: An Antidote to Chaos*, his ninth rule states, "Assume that the person you are listening to might know something you don't."[18] This, above all things, has been abandoned in higher education. By falsely assuming we know everything, we miss out on the opportunity to really learn and expand our minds, which is what a true education should be.

Currently, professors think they are the sole keepers and bearers of knowledge. The students, who are there specifically to learn from their professors, make the grave error of assuming their professor knows best. But just as every adult must face that dreadful moment when they realize their parents never had all the answers, so must college students realize that professors are stewards of education, most certainly, but they are not its arbiters.

More and more students are starting to realize this. The fact that the IDW rose to popularity so quickly speaks to this point. Young adults are thirsty for alternative points of view, and the IDW—along with the Internet in general—has provided so many alternative educational resources that college is no longer the only game in town. With such a steep price tag, many students are choosing to opt out altogether.

In 2018, college enrollment in the United States was down for the sixth straight year in a row. A recent report also shows that Gen Z is increasingly choosing trade school over a traditional college education. Combine both these stats with the fact that major job creators like Google and Apple are no longer requiring job applicants to have degrees and college no longer seems like such a wise investment for young adults.

Liberty can only exist in societies where minds are free to be open. If we want to reverse the closing of the American mind, it needs to be nurtured by allowing access to an unlimited source of knowledge and viewpoints. No one—especially not a college—has a monopoly on education. Thankfully, many young minds are opening up and understanding this to be true.

NOTES

1. Aldous Huxley, Brave New World Revisited (New York: RosettaBooks, 1958), 114.
2. Devorah Goldman, "The Closing of the Campus Mind," *The Weekly Standard*, April 6, 2015, https://www.weeklystandard.com/devorah-goldman/the-closing-of-the-campus-mind.
3. Ibid.
4. Ibid.
5. "About Us," Foundation for Individual Rights in Education, accessed May 5, 2019, https://www.thefire.org/about-us/mission/.
6. John Woodrow Cox, "Berkeley Gave Birth to the Free Speech Movement in the 1960s. Now, Conservatives are Demanding it Include Them.," *The Washington Post*, April 20, 2017, https://www.washingtonpost.com/news/retropolis/wp/2017/04/20/berkeley-gave-birth-to-the-free-speech-movement-in-the-1960s-now-conservatives-are-demanding-it-include-them/.
7. Ibid.
8. Cleve R. Wootson, Jr., "Bill Maher Doesn't Like Laura Ingraham. He Hates the Boycott of Her Show Even More.," *The Washington Post*, April 7, 2018, https://www.washingtonpost.com/news/arts-and-entertainment/wp/2018/04/07/bill-maher-doesnt-like-laura-ingraham-he-hates-the-boycott-against-her-even-more/.
9. Bari Weiss, "Meet the Renegades of the Intellectual Dark Web," *The New York Times*, May 8, 2018, https://www.nytimes.com/2018/05/08/opinion/intellectual-dark-web.html.
10. Ibid.
11. Ibid.
12. Ashe Schow, "Christina Hoff Sommers on How Academic Feminism Hurts Women," *The Washington Examiner*, September 6, 2016, https://www.

washingtonexaminer.com/christina-hoff-sommers-on-how-academic-feminism-hurts-women.

13. David French, "Unhinged Activists Never Enter the 'Real World'," *National Review*, May 26, 2017, https://www.nationalreview.com/2017/05/campus-snow-flakes-will-never-face-real-world-weinstein-sulkowicz/.

14. Abby Spegman, "Evergreen Professor at Center of Protests Resigns; College Will Pay $500,000," *Seattle Times*, September 16, 2017, https://www.seattletimes.com/seattle-news/evergreen-professor-at-center-of-protests-resigns-college-will-pay-500000/.

15. Lindsay Shepherd, Twitter, accessed May 5, 2019, https://twitter.com/NewWorldHominin/status/933057922875166720.

16. Jacob Airey, "Jordan Peterson: Dangerous People Are Teaching Your Kids," Daily Wire, June 12, 2018, https://www.dailywire.com/news/31729/jordan-pe-terson-dangerous-people-are-teaching-your-jacob-airey.

17. Barry Brownstein, "How the Closing of the Campus Mind Threatens Freedom," FEE, April 6, 2018, https://fee.org/articles/how-the-closing-of-the-campus-mind-threatens-freedom/.

18. Jordan B. Peterson, *12 Rules for Life: An Antidote to Chaos* (Canada: Random House, 2018), 233.

19. Elissa Nadworny, "Why Is Undergraduate College Enrollment Declining?," NPR, May 25, 2018, https://www.npr.org/2018/05/25/614315950/why-is-undergraduate-college-enrollment-declining.

20. Rosemary Dewar, "Generation Z Increasingly Picking Trade School over College," *Washington Examiner*, November 7, 2018, https://www.washingtonexaminer.com/red-alert-politics/generation-z-increasingly-pick-ing-trade-school-over-college.

"Learning is not attained by chance, it must be sought for with ardor and attended to with diligence."[1]

Abigail Adams

TOSS THE TEXTBOOK AND LEARN THROUGH LIVING

by Kerry McDonald

Being educated and being schooled are two completely different things. Many of us spent thousands of hours of our childhood and adolescence sitting passively in classrooms, memorizing and regurgitating information that others deemed worthy. We forgot most of it after the test, but we continued to move along the conveyor belt of institutionalized learning, confusing schooling with education. We may have been well-schooled, but what did we actually *learn*? As the best-selling author and educator, John Holt, said, "It is as true now as it was then that no matter what tests show,

---

Kerry McDonald is a Senior Education Fellow at the Foundation for Economic Education and author of the book, *Unschooled: Raising Curious, Well-Educated Children Outside the Conventional Classroom*. Find her on Twitter @kerry_edu.

very little of what is taught in school is learned, very little of what is learned is remembered, and very little of what is remembered is used. The things we learn, remember, and use are the things we seek out or meet in the daily, serious, nonschool parts of our lives."[2]

Seeking out these non-school parts of our lives that lead to real and lasting learning has never been easier or more worthwhile. Schooling arose because that was where the books and knowledge were kept. Today, knowledge is changing and accelerating at an unprecedented pace, books are widely available, and education is accessible to all of us at the click of a mouse. Disconnected from the authentic world in which we live, with a static curriculum often created years earlier, conventional schooling is as obsolete for contemporary society as the horse-and-buggy. Yet, it persists and grows under the false illusion that to be school is to be educated.

WHEN EDUCATION MEANT MORE THAN SCHOOLING

Education used to be robustly defined. Prior to the passage of compulsory school attendance laws in the mid-nineteenth century, education was considered a broad public good that was decentralized, diverse, and multifaceted. Young people became educated in a variety of ways and through an assortment of societal institutions. While different types of schools were widely available in early America, young people spent a relatively small amount of their childhood in them. They learned much of their early literacy and numeracy in their homes and throughout the communities, and they gained practical on-the-job experience through robust apprenticeship programs. In adulthood, their learning continued through vibrant workers' educational associations, the Lyceum Movement that cultivated frequent adult debates and community lectures, and a growing library system. Despite the myriad ways that people became educated prior to the introduction of centralized, compulsory schooling, the population was highly literate.[3] This informal medley of education options produced a highly educated citizenry, even for an American population brimming with slaves—who were legally banned from learning to read—and poor immigrants, and where public libraries and mass production of books were only beginning to emerge.

As state compulsory schooling laws tightened and expanded throughout the nineteenth and twentieth centuries, the variety of informal methods of education within one's wider community dwindled. Education became confined to the schoolroom and work would have to wait. As the social reformer Paul Goodman wrote, "The present expanded school systems are

coercive in their nature. The young have to attend for
various well-known reasons, none of which is necessary for their well-being or the well-being of society...
In all societies, both primitive and highly civilized,
until quite recently, most education of most children
has occurred incidentally, not in schools set aside for
the purpose."[4] In his book *Compulsory Miseducation*,
Goodman argues further that schooling can prevent
real education, and suggests that as a society we should
"multiply the paths of growing up, instead of narrowing the one existing school path."[5]

Since Goodman wrote those words in 1964, not
only have we not encouraged and supported a multi-
tude of pathways to adulthood, we have doubled down
on the "one existing school path." Today, schooling
consumes more of childhood and adolescence than
ever before in our history. Teens are working far less
and spending more time in school instead of doing real
work with real community mentors to gain real career
skills. College diplomas and, increasingly, graduate degrees, are considered mandatory markers of a "good"
education, despite their exorbitant personal and societal costs and lackluster learning results.

In his book, *The Case Against Education*, economist
Bryan Caplan argues, "First and foremost, from kinder-
garten on students spend thousands of hours study-

ing subjects irrelevant to the modern labor market."[6] While Caplan concedes that some education is useful, particularly for literacy and numeracy development, the vast quantity of schooling we as a society now consume is more about signaling than about learning. That is, the grades, diplomas, and credentials that we collect while on the vast conveyor belt of schooling signal to employers such qualities as intelligence, work ethic, and conformity that they may value and that can be difficult for them to assess in other ways. Indeed, a 2017 Accenture/Harvard Business School study found that degree inflation—that is, new degree requirements for jobs that previously didn't require them—is soaring.[7] Schooling may be a shortcut for employers but it can be a long, tedious, unfulfilling, and increasingly costly pursuit for individuals.

ALTERNATIVE SIGNALS

As a boy, Ansel Adams was an energetic child. His teachers grew increasingly frustrated by his restlessness and exuberance. They told his father that Ansel needed more discipline, but his father disagreed. He thought Ansel needed more freedom. When Ansel was 12, his father removed him from school and enabled him to learn at home in a mostly self-directed way. At first, Ansel taught himself to play the piano and began to take in-home piano lessons to fine-tune his skills. His initial career was working as a professional musician, but when he was a teenager he received a camera as a gift and couldn't shake his passion for photography. While performing as a musician, Ansel nurtured his emerging talent for photography and enhanced his skills. He read widely, devouring photography magazines and learning darkroom techniques. He connected with local camera clubs and attended their meetings, and he visited numerous photography and art exhibits.

Ansel frequently visited Yosemite Valley, the national park that would shape his photography for the rest of his life. He joined the Sierra Club and became friends with many of the club's leaders. These relationships led to early opportunities to have his photographs published in Sierra Club bulletins, which then led to further photography commissions and numerous published books. Ansel ultimately gave up his career in music to devote himself full-time to photography, becoming the most renowned American landscape photographer of the 20th century.

Ansel's story shows the power of an emerging interest combined with deliberate efforts to practice and perfect one's abilities in that interest area. It also shows that to make a living doing what one likes to do, there needs to be a market. For Ansel, finding a market meant improving his skills, learning from others, volunteering, making connections, and building relationships that led to an initial opportunity to showcase his work in a respected publication that sought good photography. Understanding market demand, and leveraging interests and abilities to meet that demand, is the key to turning what one likes to do into a fulfilling career. Ansel Adams made a career switch, jettisoning his job as a formally trained and accomplished musician to become a budding photographer. He didn't go to school to be a photographer, nor did he collect degrees and credentials; he practiced and refined his craft, volunteered, cultivated personal and professional relationships, and seized market opportunities. In short, Ansel found an alternative signal to represent his worth to potential employers. Once he had that initial job opportunity, he continued to pursue his interest, improve his abilities, and seize the next market demand moment.

The opportunity for transforming interests and abilities into marketable skills that lead to rewarding careers without college has never been easier. Ansel Adams was operating in an analog world of self-education when information and knowledge were static and harder to access. Today, if one wants to learn photography, there is a host of dynamic, online, in-depth courses such as those offered by learning platforms like Lynda.com, available for free through most public libraries. There is an extensive online community of other photographers, including those who are far more experienced and willing to share their expertise. Instead of being a fixed and stable process, photography is now an active, technology-driven, constantly changing art form with a host of different mediums and markets. While learning from books can still be helpful and inspirational to a budding photographer, learning through an array of digital resources and online networks may be even more valuable.

The vast technological platform that is now at our fingertips makes self-education accessible to all. It also makes clunkier forms of learning, like sitting passively in a classroom memorizing and regurgitating information from textbooks and a predetermined curriculum, seem passé at best. The true gift of technology is that it supports natural curiosity and enables self-education in ways never thought possible. Humans have an instinctual drive to learn and are able to learn an incredible amount of knowledge and skill in their earliest years. This natural curiosity continues into adulthood, but is often dulled by a forced system of education that prioritizes schooling over learning. The ability to self-educate can be schooled out of us, leaving us dependent on others to be taught. Technology changes the relationship between teaching and learning. It empowers the learner, supports the rapid change of knowledge creation, and lets the learner decide what to learn, when, and from whom. Learners may still choose to be taught, but their teachers work for them.

MINIMALLY INVASIVE EDUCATION

In 1999, Sugata Mitra led an experiment in an Indian slum of Kalkaji, Delhi that would disrupt what we have come to know about education and learning. While working in his office building adjacent to the poor village, Mitra wondered what would happen if he placed a computer on the outside wall of his office for the children of the village to freely play with and explore. It turns out, a lot would happen. The children, most of whom were illiterate and all of whom had never seen a computer before, flocked to this new device. Mitra offered no help or guidance but simply said the children could play with it if they wanted to. Over the next several days and weeks, the children taught themselves and became highly computer literate. Within the first few hours, they learned how to surf the Internet. They then learned how to download and record music, create graphics, and send and receive email messages. They soon taught themselves some English and explored English-language websites.

Mitra, who was trained as a physicist but is now an education professor at Newcastle University, coined his project the "Hole in the Wall" experiment and replicated it in dozens of other urban and rural poor locations throughout India, all with the same results. In one experiment, Mitra found that children in an Indian fishing village taught themselves the basics of biotechnology—in English—with no help from teachers. Within six months, test scores of these self-taught children were practically equivalent to the scores of children in India's elite private schools.[8] Mitra found that young people have an astonishing capacity to self-educate, particularly with technology as a learning platform, when they are provided with safe, public access and allowed to work collaboratively with their peers. Mitra calls his approach Minimally Invasive Education, or maximum learning with minimum instruction. In 2013, Mitra won the $1 million TED prize for his TED talk detailing his work and findings.

In further studies, Mitra and his colleagues discovered that not only did children effectively teach themselves a high degree of content, they also taught themselves just as well as children who were taught in a conventional classroom with a traditional teacher. In a 2005 journal article, Mitra explained the results of his large-scale study of children ages six to 14 in India, comparing the computer literacy skills of children who were self-taught versus children who were traditionally taught. He found that the skills of both groups were equivalent, with the self-taught children just as capable as the classroom-trained children. Mitra and his research team concluded that children's natural curiosity and eagerness to explore the world around them lead to successful and lasting learning, independent of a classroom and a teacher.[9]

NOT JUST CHILDREN

It's not just children who have this powerful capacity to teach themselves using the tools around them. Adults can do this too—if we reclaim the natural learning tendencies we all possessed as young children before schooling diminished them. Boston College psychology professor Peter Gray studies how humans learn. He found that schooling is what turns off our instinctual learning drives. In his book, *Free To Learn*, Gray writes:

> Children come into the world burning to learn and genetically programmed with extraordi-

nary capacities for learning. They are little
learning machines. Within their first four years
or so they absorb an unfathomable amount of
information and skills without any instruction... Nature does not turn off this enormous
desire and capacity to learn when children turn
five or six. We turn it off with our coercive system of schooling.[10]

Gray researches how young people learn without
conventional schooling, and how they turn out in adulthood. He has found that these "unschoolers" maintain
and cultivate their self-direction, are capable of learning what they need to know when they need to know
it, and pursue whatever career goals they wish, often
tied to interests that began to emerge in childhood
and adolescence. Most notably, more than half of the
grown "unschoolers" he surveyed in one of his studies
worked as entrepreneurs. And the longer or more continuously they were unschooled, the more likely it was
that they became entrepreneurs.[11]

In many ways, the work of researchers like Mitra and
Gray flip the previous understanding of adult learning
on its head. Rather than suggesting that adults learn
differently from children, the research of self-taught
and unschooled young people shows that many of the
qualities associated with adult learners are really the

qualities of human learners more generally when freed from a schooled mindset. The well-known pioneer in the area of adult learning theory, Malcolm Knowles, posited six theories of adult learning including (1) that adults need to know the reason, the "why," for learning something; (2) that adults move toward self-directed learning as they mature, demanding more control over their learning; (3) that mounting experience allows for greater learning, as adults build on previously-acquired knowledge; (4) that learning becomes more directly related to one's social roles in adulthood; (5) that adults focus more on immediate use of knowledge to solve specific problems and address current issues, rather than accumulating subject-based knowledge for some amorphous future purpose; and (6) that the motivation to learn becomes more internal as one ages.[12]

Many of these characteristics of adult learners are also characteristics of "unschooled" children, or those who learned in self-directed education environments in their youth. Indeed, these are qualities of learning that babies and young children exhibit all the time. A child learning to walk, for example, is highly self-directed and internally motivated in her task. She uses past experiences to refine her attempts, leverages the support of people egging her on, and strives to walk to meet her purposes. These qualities remain when they are not turned off by coercive schooling. They can also be reignited in adulthood when we escape the confines of the classroom. We must learn what we already knew in our earliest days: that learning is a natural human process driven by personal goals, past and present experiences, and an internal motivation to understand and master the world.

BECOMING A SELF-DIRECTED LEARNER

To move from a schooled mindset of learning to an unschooled one takes some deliberate effort. After all, most have spent their childhood and adolescence being told what to read, write, and do. It may take conscientious effort for someone to begin to read the books he wants to read, write what he wants to write, and do the work he wants to do. This is not to imply that one will never again do unappealing things or take on delegated tasks. It means that now there is a choice of whether or not to do certain things in pursuit of one's self-directed goals.

For Karen Leong, being a self-directed learner was what enabled her to nurture her passion for cake design and launch a thriving custom cake decorating business. When she was 11, she began exploring cake design techniques on YouTube and used that technology platform to build and refine her skills. Those You-Tube videos got her started and prompted her to take more formal classes, including a 5-month cake decorating course and a 9-month course in French pastry art. At 18, she hit a crossroads: should she go to college or launch a cake design business? She chose the latter, putting off college indefinitely while she expands her cake business, hires employees, teaches cake design classes to both adults and children, and wins awards for her artistic and culinary talents.[13]

CALCULATING THE TRUE COSTS OF COLLEGE

Maybe Karen will decide to go to college someday in pursuit of some specific goal, or maybe she won't. Questioning the value of college, and challenging the assumption that one must go to college at a certain age in a certain brick-and-mortar space, can be an important step in taking charge of one's learning and livelihood. There may be no compelling reason to enroll in college at age 18 and pursue a specific degree track that may not be personally meaningful. Societal pressure, or following the mantra that this is "what everyone does," can lead to costly years spent pursuing a shallow piece of paper, with no clear idea of what one is truly capable of doing for a career. Too many leave college with a diploma but without the passion, skills, or personal agency that lead to fulfilling work.

Beyond the out-of-pocket financial costs of college, which today can bury graduates in mountains of debt that lock them into jobs they may not like just so they can pay off student loans, there are other costs of college to consider. The big cost of college is its opportunity cost, or the cost of the possibilities one foregoes while attending college. If Karen, the cake designer, chose the college path instead of the entrepreneurial one, she would have paid both the monetary costs of college tuition along with the cost of the foregone earnings she had accumulated while growing her business. Her true cost of college, then, would have been significantly higher than the college's price tag. Additionally, Karen may have other hidden costs of attending college, such as the mental anguish of wondering what running her business might have been like and the lost opportunity to develop critical entrepreneurial skills and business savvy. One could argue that Karen could have gone to college and then launched her business, but that doesn't fully capture the current financial and opportunity costs of that decision. And, if she decides to attend college at some future point, she will enter college with more skills, more financial stability from her company's earnings, and a clearer focus on what the purpose of college would be for her specific life goals.

ALTERNATIVES TO COLLEGE

To get off the conveyor belt of forced schooling to college to career requires some guts. It takes an understanding of the true costs of college, which can outweigh the benefits, and it takes an eagerness to be in charge of your own education and career. In short, you need to be the leader of your own life, rather than being led along a well-worn, costly, and often unsatisfying college and career path. If you decide college is for you—it meets your personal and professional goals and the benefits outweigh the costs—then go! But if you're uncertain of the benefits of college and hesitant about the costs—then wait! There is always time to go to college if you want, whether attending on-campus as a residential student or in one of the many top-quality online college degree programs that provide similar credentials with fewer costs.

If you decide to wait, or to skip college altogether, what's next? Here are five ideas for creating an alternative pathway to a meaningful career without college.

1. Set Micro-Goals

A key first step in planning your alternative career path is to internalize the belief that you are not simply rejecting college, you are embracing something different, something better. This isn't about turning down opportunities, it's about seeking and creating new ones. You are moving toward something great.

Part of this shift in thinking requires you to pull out your figurative compass and determine in which direction you should start walking. To move forward you don't necessarily need a defined end goal or vision of the ideal career, though it's great if you can; you simply need to have some micro-goals to start you on your path.

What are some small, simple, achievable micro-goals to get you going? One micro-goal might be to take a computer skills class at your local library to get more proficient in Microsoft Excel. Another micro-goal might be to take a local adult education class or an online course on a topic you really care about. A third micro-goal might be to create a website or write a daily blog that catalogs your efforts, accomplishments, and setbacks. A fourth micro-goal might be to seek out apprenticeship opportunities, and so on. The specific micro-goal you set is not as important as the act of setting these small goals, working diligently toward achieving them, and using them to adjust your compass as you continue on your distinct pathway.

2. Find Mentors

Along with goal-setting comes relationship-building. Begin networking with people who are working in jobs or pursuing careers related to your interests. Share your interest in their work and ask if they would grant you a few minutes of their time to talk about how they found their career, what skills they think are most valuable, and if they have suggestions for where you should go next. Send a thank you note or email and keep in touch with these mentors, building trust and connection over time.

Mentors can be peers, too. The proliferation of online communities and other informal networks can facilitate your connection with like-minded peers and influential mentors, including those who may be a step further along on your desired career path. Without the age segregation so characteristic of schooling and college, learning outside the classroom is more organic and authentic. Your mentors could be much younger than you, but much more experienced in the areas you most care about. Be on the lookout for mentors of all ages and stages.

3. Learn

Take charge of your own learning by reading as much as you can about the topics and careers that interest you. As a self-directed learner, no one is going to tell you what to learn or do. You need to take your own education very seriously, reading books and articles to expand your knowledge and leveraging all available resources to build your skills. According to the World Economic Forum, many of today's top careers and job skills didn't even exist five or ten years ago. And robots are increasingly performing the jobs that humans once did. Staying ahead of trends, continuously building high-demand skills, and watching out for opportunities can help you build a rewarding, challenging career. With a vast technological platform at your fingertips, you have limitless access to everything you could possibly want or need to learn. Maximize this platform to move from a schooled mindset to a learning one, where you are the master of your own education and career.

4. Do

One of my favorite sayings is, "Who reads and reads and does not what he knows is he who plows and plows and never sows."

It's not enough to learn, you also need to *do*. As you pursue your alternatives to college, get working! Seek unpaid and volunteer opportunities, perhaps as a side gig while you work for money in another job. Offer to be an intern. Start a business, as an ancillary project or as a full-time endeavor. If you want to be a writer, then start writing! Perfect your craft, draft an array of articles, and submit them to a variety of online and print publications. A primary reason why you are choosing to skip college is so that you can pursue meaningful work *now*. If that work is not meaningful or useful in moving you further along your career path, then the opportunity costs of college are not so high and you may need to reconsider your approach. But if, instead, you skip college so you can *do*, then start *doing!*

Companies today are beginning to recognize that college diplomas can be empty signals of competence. Some, including high-tech giants like IBM, Google, and Apple, and retailers like Home Depot, Starbucks, and Whole Foods, don't require a college degree to gain entry into a strong career track with upward potential. Driven by a tight labor market and a dearth of talented workers, more companies are valuing real skills over hollow signals. In a 2017 interview with CNBC, an IBM vice president said that about 15 percent of the company's employees do not have a college degree.

Instead, IBM seeks workers with value-added skills
gained through experiences like coding boot camps or
industry-focused vocational classes.[14]

Seize as many opportunities as possible to do the
work you want to be doing. This may involve narrowing
your interests and specializing your skills, and weeding
out work that doesn't suit you to find the work that
does. Through this process, you will gain competencies, connections, and a clarity of purpose that will be
essential as you launch your career.

5. Adapt and Improve

Self-education requires you to adapt to changing
circumstances and demands and to strive for con-
tinuous improvement. Be agile. If the career path you
were set on dries up or isn't quite what you expected,
then shift course. If robots and automation have tak-
en over your field of interest, then look elsewhere.
Embrace the unknown and welcome change. Learning what you don't like or what you're not good at
can be just as valuable as learning what you like or
excel at—maybe even more so! With these changes
will come new opportunities for self-improvement
and new possibilities to explore. Maybe you need to
go back to step one and create some new or different

micro-goals. Maybe you need to meet new people or learn new things. Be flexible and open to what comes next. Your learning never ends.

It is possible for you to skip college, toss the textbook, and learn through living. It's also important to realize that textbooks aren't the problem, *per se*. Sometimes it can be great to learn from a textbook! The important thing to remember as you chart a career and life path without college is that you are the one driving the process. This sounds like such a simple point: *Of course, I'm in charge of my life and learning!* But years of schooling can convince even the most self-directed among us to question our ability to self-educate and to doubt our agency. We were taught to be taught, so we learned to be led. Unraveling that myth can be far harder than it seems. By separating your education from your schooling, you can regain control of your own learning and recognize the many ways you can learn from the people, places, and things around you. You can set goals, seek mentors, pursue knowledge, jump into the work you want to be doing, and adapt and improve along the way.

The American entrepreneur and author Jim Rohn famously said, "Formal education will make you a living; self-education will make you a fortune." Taking the reins of your own learning will fill you with confidence, clarity, and enthusiasm that may have been weakened during your years of formal education. Learning through living, in pursuit of your distinct passions and career ambitions, can open a world of possibility and set you on the path toward a rewarding life and livelihood.

NOTES

1. Letter to John Quincy Adams, May 8, 1780.
2. John Holt, *How Children Fail* (New York: Merloyd Lawrence, 1982), 232.
3. David Tyack, *The One Best System: A History of American Urban Education* (Cambridge: Harvard University Press, 1974), 66.
4. Paul Goodman, *New Reformation: Notes of a Neolithic Conservative* (New York: Random House, 1970), 67–68.
5. Ibid, 87.
6. Bryan Caplan, *The Case Against Education: Why the Education System Is a Waste of Time and Money* (Princeton: Princeton University Press, 2018), 10.
7. J. Fuller and M. Raman, et al., "Dismissed By Degrees," Harvard Business School, October 2017, http://www.hbs.edu/managing-the-future-of-work/Documents/dismissed-by-degrees.pdf.
8. Monica Martinez, "Undeveloped World Taps Technology for Learning," *The Phi Delta Kappan, vol. 92, no. 7*, 2011, 70–71.
9. Sugata Mitra, et al., "Acquisition of Computer Literacy on Shared Public Computers: Children and the 'Hole in the Wall.'" *Australasian Journal of Educational Technology 21, no. 3*, 2005, 407–426.
10. Peter Gray, *Free to Learn: Why Unleashing the Instinct to Play Will Make Our Children Happier, More Self-Reliant, and Better Learners for Life* (New York: Basic Books, 2013), x–xi.
11. Peter Gray, "A Survey of Grown Unschooler I: Overview of Findings," Freedom To Learn, Psychology Today, June 7, 2014, https://www.psychologytoday.com/us/blog/freedom-learn/201406/survey-grown-unschoolers-i-overview-findings.
12. Malcolm Knowles, et al., *The Adult Learner: The Definitive Classic in Adult Education and Human*

Resource Development, 6th edition (Boston: Elsevier Inc., 2005).

13. Oon Yeoh, "The Unschooled Cake Designer." *New Straits Times*, January 27, 2018, https://www.nst.com.my/lifestyle/pulse/2018/01/329262/unschooled-cake-designer.

14. Courtney Connley, "Google, Apple and 12 Other Companies that No Longer Require Employees to Have a College Degree," CNBC, October 8, 2018, https://www.cnbc.com/2018/08/16/15-companies-that-no-longer-require-employees-to-have-a-college-degree.html.

"Actually, all education is self-education. A teacher is only a guide, to point out the way, and no school, no matter how excellent, can give you education. What you receive is like the outlines in a child's coloring book. You must fill in the colors yourself."[1]

Louis L'Amour

DITCH THE DIPLOMA

BUILD A PORTFOLIO
EMPLOYERS CARE ABOUT

by Isaac Morehouse

"Dude, I'm so hungover. I don't even remember what happened last night. I want to puke. So, wanna get schwasted again tonight?"

Two guys next to me. A typical 9:15 AM, Tuesday class. That's when it hit me.

I scanned the beige cinder-block cell, the epilepsy-inducing flicker of fluorescent lights overhead. The piece of paper in my hand had a barely-legible collection of spelling and grammatical errors. It was a "trade and grade" exercise. How was I supposed to assign an arbitrary letter of the alphabet to this chicken scratch?

Isaac Morehouse is the CEO of Crash, the career launch platform, and the founder of Praxis, the startup apprenticeship program. He's dedicated to the relentless pursuit of freedom and has written over 1,000 articles and eight books. You can find him at isaacmorehouse.com.

Arbitrary letters—that's what hit me. I would leave here after a few years and more money spent than I'd care to admit. I'd go out into the world with a resume. It would include the same letters as everyone else slouching in this classroom. "B.A."

All I was really buying was a piece of paper that mumbled, "On average, I'm probably no worse than everyone else with this same piece of paper." Including, eventually, my hungover classmates.

That was a pretty weak way to sell myself on the job market. There's got to be something better.

YOU NEED A SIGNAL

In that moment, I stumbled upon what economists call the "signaling theory" of education. In a nutshell: You don't go to college to learn. Abundant evidence shows that learning doesn't really happen, even for the subjects studied. And the subjects studied are almost entirely irrelevant to success in the real world, personal or professional. You go to college to get a signal.

The piece of paper conferred upon graduation is the product. It is the entire product. Not the classes, or sports, or parties, or social networking, or any other stuff associated with the college bundle. All those things could be had for free. Anyone could move to a college town, sit in on classes without registering, go to parties, and all the rest. But people don't do this. They register. The other stuff may be an added benefit (or an added cost, as in the case of classes. Everyone's happy when they're canceled.) The paper is why people pay.

The paper is a signal, and signals are valuable. But the degree is a particular kind of signal that is now dead. Most people don't realize it yet. The sooner you understand this, the better you'll be. The degree signal is only valuable in the absence of something better. That something better is possible, and it's vastly cheaper, faster, more effective, and more fun.

THE CREDENTIAL ECONOMY

The 20th century was the century of the credential. The "Organization Man" dominated the career landscape. Individuals became absorbed into the collective blob of corporate identity. Career and company were one and the same. Jump through all the right hoops, follow all the right rules, and you would slowly move up the prefabricated ranks of a single organization until you retire.

That sounds pretty awful to modern ears. But it was actually a big improvement over the career model of previous centuries. There was more wealth and stability. The point isn't to rip on the past, only to make sure we don't act like we still live there when the world has moved on.

The credential played a key role in the 20th-century economy. Information was hard to come by. As jobs became more complex and companies larger, managers had to hire complete strangers and entrust them with important stuff. But if we've never met, how can I tell you're legit?

A prospective employee could lie about their abilities. It'd be difficult to find out they were lying until it was too late. Employers needed something that signaled a basic level of ability and work ethic, especially for managerial roles. Degrees did the trick.

A college degree is like a stamp of approval from an old, established institution on a young, unknown worker. It says, "Whatever else is true of this person, they made it through our system and we're comfortable staking our reputation on theirs." You can see how this would lower the information costs of employers. Rather than needing to verify that someone is reasonably competent, hardworking, and trustworthy, they could let a third party validate it for them.

It became clear that buying a degree was one of the better ways to signal employability for certain roles. Then the government started subsidizing higher learning. A lot. A whole lot. Then everyone began to want a degree as a symbol of not just employability, but social status. Then colleges started aggressively expanding and lining up for the gravy train of goodies, courtesy of unwilling taxpayers. Then the degree-equals-employ-ability narrative moved from one based on correlation to one based on unquestioned, religious-level devotion.

First, the better-off, higher-quality young people flocked to college, but the increase of subsidies for colleges increased the number of spaces and soon it became common for the more mediocre talent to attend. The perceived correlation between degrees and as the cause of better-quality workers persisted because more of the better workers happened to have degrees, but the correlation got weaker and weaker over time—and it was never causation. By the start of the 21st century, there were so many holders of so many degrees from so many institutions that there was at least as much noise as signal in the degree economy.

This had a perverse effect on the college experience, too. The more people flocked to it as nothing more than a magical job ticket, the worse the environment for learning anything valuable. Everybody cheers when class is canceled because they aren't there for learning but for a piece of paper. For most, bad mindsets and bad habits form during a five-year, booze-fueled binge that's more about avoiding productive adult life than growing into it effectively. Even if tuition was zero, the opportunity cost and the cost of an avoidant, reactive, least-common-denominator mindset are enough to make college a bad way to prepare for a career.

The 20th-century model was simple. Your resume was what got you an interview. You stacked your resume with third-party brands to signal your ability, then shot it out among the hundreds or thousands of other resumes, hoping the right collection of bullets kept you from getting culled from the stack by a check-listing HR department.

By the 21st century, the proliferation of third-party credentials for sale meant hardly any of them meant anything anymore.

But something else happened. It wasn't just that the supply of third-party credentials inflated to the point that they lost signaling power. It was also that demand emerged for new and better information. Information that had previously been impossible to obtain.

The insane market for third-party approval stamps came about because getting better information was hard. But thanks to the Internet, it's now easy.

THE MAKER ECONOMY

You are what you make.

Until recently, there wasn't a way to show what you can make unless you happened to work with your hands. Most careers now involve working with people and information. How can you demonstrate to people that you can make excellent processes for managing multiple competing tasks, streamlining event preparations, and getting several parties on the same page quickly?

Maybe that was hard once, but today it's easy.

You have at your fingertips the greatest tool for conveying information the world has ever known. And it gets better every day. You can build something that blows a degree away and makes you exponentially more impressive and attractive to employers than a stale, static credential. Degrees are an expensive way to convey information. Today, information is free.

I said degrees are dead, whether or not most people know it yet. The Internet killed them. But it didn't kill them by putting lectures and courses online—remember, people don't pay tuition for the lectures and courses. The Internet killed degrees because it made the cost of information so low that now anyone anywhere can build a better signal than a degree through a digital footprint, brand, or body of work.

You can now be your own credential. You can make something better than a third-party paper.

Everyone is a maker now. The credential economy was about buying someone else's proof of your baseline ability. The maker economy is about building your own proof of your ability.

Don't believe me? Let's compare two applicants for an entry level marketing job.

APPLICANT A

The first applicant is 22 years-old. He spent five years and six figures in school. He now has $30,000 in debt and no real-world skills. He needs to start earning decent money fast and get a job respectable enough to keep his parents off his back. It's a race against time. He starts scanning job boards upon graduation. He follows the rules in the "Marketing Associate at Acme, Inc." job posting and sends a resume. The condensed version:

- BA in Marketing from State University, 3.4 GPA
- Played intramural rugby
- Volunteered one summer at a soup kitchen

His resume goes in the stack with 427 others.

APPLICANT B

The second applicant is 18. She hasn't spent a dime on or a day in college. She did spend the summer setting up a blog, subscribing to the marketing email lists of a dozen different companies, reading the emails they sent her, and writing a post every day for 30 days about what she liked and didn't like about their efforts to sell to her. Then she made a 1-minute video summarizing the key takeaways for good marketing emails.

She identified a few companies she really likes, spent a few hours researching their products, customers, social media presence, and team members.

She didn't look at job postings. Instead, she sent this email to the team members she thought would be most relevant based on their title and social media presence:

Dear Jim and Jane,

I love your company! I've been using your product for a few months now and it's excellent, and I'm a big fan of the wonderful brand you've built.

I went through your social media accounts and came up with three ideas to increase customer engagement:

- Create shareable images for each weekly deal (I've attached one that I created, feel free to use it)

- Ask a question each week about features people would like and engage with their comments

- Create "behind the scenes" short videos, text, and images showing the process of creating the product and humanize the team and company more

I would love to do all of the above and more for you. I would like to do it completely free for one month to prove my ability and show dramatic improvement in social engagement and new customers.

You can check out my personal website here, where I have a project showing my process of learning about digital marketing.

Thanks for your time, and I look forward to hearing from you!

Her email gets passed around in amazement, and the team tries to figure out the best person to interview her.

It's painfully obvious who built a better signal of their ability and interest. Yet Applicant B did all of this for free in a matter of months, while A went deep into debt and spent half a decade of his life. How many applications before he gets an interview? How many attempts before Applicant B gets one? It's not even close.

And consider that she has no debt, a five-year headstart, less pressure and expectation at such a young age and that she can experiment, work for cheap or free to get started, and be more flexible. If she's already sending a better signal after just a few months of effort, imagine how much further ahead she'll be when she's the same age as Applicant A and has five full years of professional experience?

"WHAT HAVE YOU DONE FOR ME LATELY?"

Sure, the girl who built a better signal might have the edge nabbing that first professional opportunity, especially if she offers to apprentice or work for free to start. But what happens next? What if, a year or two down the road, she wants to move up—won't her lack of degree hurt her then?

Nope.

You're only as good as the last most interesting thing you've done. Once you have tangible, provable experience creating value, no one cares about your schooling.

Once you have a college degree, no one asks about your high school diploma. Once you have real work experience, no one asks about your degree. In fact, once you have anything more interesting and valuable no one cares. If your degree is the most interesting thing about you, you're in trouble.

Imagine Applicant B crushing it for a few years in her marketing role, impressing everyone she works with, and then pitching herself for a marketing manager role she's proven she's ready for. How many managers would say, "You know, she creates a ton of value, and has an amazing track record, and has proven her ability to do this job we need to be done, but let's spend a bunch of time and money finding and training someone new, because she didn't go to college"? Only those who want to lose to the competition would ever think this way.

Sure, there's an odd status-worshipper here and there who will play power games about credential pedigree, but those people are not the kind you want to work with anyway, and companies that reward that are rare and getting rarer. An ambitious, creative person will fly by the status politickers in the world of value creation. Let them coddle the precious paper while you build awesome stuff and delight customers and coworkers.

Like it or not, you can't cling to the past and hope it propels you into the future. You need to be growing and creating every single day and building a body of work that proves it. No one cares what you did two years ago if what you did last year is awesome.

Don't look back—move forward.

HOW TO HACK THE FIRST STEP

Here's the most important takeaway from this chapter: There are only two things that matter when it comes to career success:

1. Your ability to create value
2. Your ability to prove it

Notice what's not listed: How special you are as a human being. How much you think you deserve it. How proud your mom is of you. How many years you studied. How prestigious your background, grades, or any other fluff is.

None of that stuff matters unless it directly contributes to points 1 and 2.

This means there are only two fronts on which to advance. Put all your energy into improving these two things, and you'll win.

When you're first getting started on your career, you don't have a ton of skill and ability to create value, nor do you have a lot of proof for the value you can create. So how do you convince people to take a chance on you? Lower the cost, raise the value.

LOWER THE COST WITH FREE WORK

Lowering the cost of working with you means you need to make it easy for employers to say yes to giving you a shot. This can happen in a lot of ways. The obvious one is to lower the financial cost. Since you know you're low on skill and experience, offer to work for cheap or free to prove yourself.

There's something funny that happens in some people's brain when they hear the idea of working for free as a great way to launch a career. They think it's offensive. They think it's exploitation. They think doing work and learning valuable real-world on-the-job skills for no money is unfair. Yet these very same people find it perfectly acceptable for young people with no skills to pay tens of thousands of dollars to sit in classrooms and not learn anything valuable for their careers while also not earning money. Ignore them. They don't get it.

Launching a career is not free. There is always a cost. You've got to put in time, effort, and money to build skills, build a signal, build a network, build experiences, and get people's attention for that first job. It turns out that free work is probably the least expensive way to do these things. Working for free is a better deal for you than almost any other approach.

RAISE THE VALUE WITH COMPARATIVE ADVANTAGE

The great thing about having little skill or experience is that you have a secret weapon: your low opportunity cost. Opportunity cost is the value of the next best activity you could be doing. An unskilled 18-year-old has a very low opportunity cost. That means they can overcome their lack of skill and experience by using this secret weapon.

When you start your career, almost everyone else has a higher opportunity cost than you. If you can find low-value activities that high-value people are doing, you can offer to take those on and free them up. Even if you're not that great at them, they may bite.

Say you do everything worse than the person you want to work for. They may still want to hire you if you can exploit your comparative advantage. Your comparative advantage is the difference between your opportunity cost and someone else's. Imagine a busy

CEO who is great at scheduling his own travel. Even if you're worse at travel scheduling, his opportunity cost is so high—the hour it takes him to schedule travel can be used doing more valuable things—that you can take on his scheduling and still create value even if it takes you twice as long.

WHAT SKILLS?

To build skills that can create value, identify areas where your interests and abilities intersect with the things people value. Actually, scratch that. "Interests" and "abilities" are too restrictive. You need more experience before you really have a clear idea of what those are. Start even easier. Start with "stuff I don't hate" and "stuff I don't suck at."

Think of a Venn diagram. One circle is stuff you don't hate, one is stuff you don't suck at, and the third is stuff other people value enough to pay for it. The intersection of those three is where you start. You don't need to "find your passion" or calling right away. That's too hard and it will probably change as you gain experience and knowledge. The perfect fit for you probably doesn't exist yet. You might have to create it. So, get started where the three circles intersect, build some skills in those areas, and take any and every opportunity that you don't hate and don't suck at.

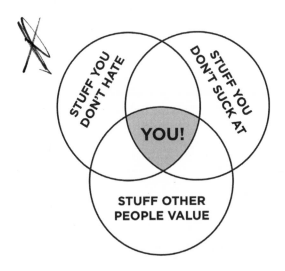

HOW TO BUILD SKILLS

When it comes to building skills, real-world projects beat books and lectures. Humans learn best when solving real problems. We learn to the task, not the test. So if you want to build your graphic design skills, for example, don't start by consuming, start by creating. Don't read or watch info on how to do it, instead give yourself a real project with a real due date. Promise a friend you'll create a logo for his website in two weeks. Then give it a try. Now that you have a real problem to solve with real obstacles you'll encounter along the way, those instructional videos on how to do it will have context and value to you.

HOW TO SIGNAL SKILLS: SHOW DON'T TELL

When it comes to proving the value you can create, it's not enough to tell people. The résumé is a 500-year-old piece of technology. A static list of qualifications on paper is hardly the cutting edge of signals of your ability to create value. Sure, now you can turn it into a PDF and send it around, but it's still a paperbound list of words that requires people to trust you or whatever certifications you list.

Today we have something much better. You wouldn't use a horse and buggy if you were in a hurry to get across town, so why use a piece of paper to get a career started? Use the best available technology.

It's only really been a few years since pretty much anyone anywhere began to have the ability to do things like shoot, edit, and share a quality video. That means the first movers, those who make the best use of the new and better information technology, will have big advantages.

A piece of paper that says, "Skills: Microsoft Excel," communicates nothing compared to a two-minute video of you sharing your screen and talking through how you created a pivot table and used some advanced functions to display data in Excel.

Real-world projects are not only the best way to build skills, but they're also the best way to signal those skills. If you want to signal your ability to work hard, stay disciplined, and communicate clearly, a 30-day daily blogging challenge does more than just telling people.

Ideally, for any skill you want to signal, pick a time-bound project, learn out loud as you complete it, then create a nice short summary blog post and video to share what you did and what you learned.

HOW TO SELL THOSE SKILLS AND SIGNAL

It's not enough to build skills and build a signal of those skills and hope, like in the movie *Field of Dreams*, that "they will come." You need to take the initiative. You are in the driver's seat!

The passive, generic resume blast to job postings approach is dying, and it will take you with it.

You'll dramatically increase your odds of launching a great career with your newfound skill and signal if you follow these steps:

- Pick 5-10 companies you would love to work for.

- Start with one and do a deep dive into every-thing about their products, customers, team, mission, culture, history, etc. Take as much time as you need. Could be hours, days, or even weeks if they have lots of content.
- Create a list of 2-3 things you think you could do that would create value for them. Even highly specific stuff for just one team member is OK. "I can schedule you on a podcast every week" might appeal to some!
- Check their job listings and if they have any roles, or even parts of roles, that might fit in your Venn diagram of things you don't hate and things you don't suck at, format your pitch around it. If not, don't let it stop you! Many great jobs aren't advertised.
- Choose a project that creates value for the com-pany, even if they don't hire you, and complete it.
- Pick the best person or persons at the company to contact and dig around or guess until you find their email address.
- Send a clear email that focuses first and fore-most on how much you love their company, showing your genuine interest. Use the dat-ing analogy: If you want a date, you don't list the three reasons you are highly date-able. You

tell the person what you find fascinating about
them! Companies are no different. "I'd make a
good employee" is weak compared to "I'm in
love with your mission."

- In the email, share something you created for
  them for free and say you'd love to do more like
  that and are happy to do so on a free trial period to prove yourself.
- Let them know you appreciate their time either
  way!
- Rinse, and repeat for each of the companies on
  your list.
- Ten of those will get more in return than 100
  résumé-based applications.

BYE-BYE "ORGANIZATION MAN"

Hello "Me, Inc."

The world of work is changing fast. We may be
nearing the *End of Jobs*, to borrow the title of a great
book by Taylor Pearson. Large institutions are less and
less important in the economy, and individuals have
more power, autonomy, and value. It's easier than ever
to do contract work, project-based work, short-term
gigs, freelance, or start your own company.

This makes college even more detrimental. Forget the useless factual stuff in the lectures. All the habits and mindsets are the opposite of those valued in the 21st-century economy. Following rules, suffering monotony, jumping through hoops, being valued for arbitrary obedience instead of real-world value creation, and being told exactly how to "win" ahead of time are the antithesis of the ways to succeed in the market today.

Some people think that a good, stable job with a title at a large corporation is safer than, say, working at a high growth startup that may fail in the next 18-months. They are wrong. That rote corporate job is under constant and growing pressure from software and machines. Most accounting and bookkeeping, for example, will likely be automated, and probably sooner than we expect. If your ability to earn money is completely chained to one narrow skillset in one specific company in one city, the way line workers at the automakers were, then if the role or company goes under, so do you.

If you work at a brand new, venture-backed startup, frantically trying to grow, even if it fails in 18 months as many do, you don't. Startup founders and employees create or work for other startups. They disperse when one company fails, and three new ones are born. An inside sales rep at one software startup has more opportunity at ten other startups than anyone chained to the tight corporate structure of one megacorp.

Not to mention the increasing value of entrepreneurship. Whether or not you ever start a company, today you need to think of yourself as an entrepreneur. *The Startup of You*, to borrow another book title.

That mean you should focus early and often on building the skills and mindsets that are applicable across the board. The things uniquely human, that aren't threatened by automation but enhanced by it. Creative problem solving, innovation, adaptability, experimentation, curiosity, persistence, communication, and unique intersections of both "soft" and "hard" skills.

Strange as it may sound, the more secure career path may be the more risky, open-ended, and experimental.

BE YOUR OWN CREDENTIAL

You no longer need to appeal to third-party institutions to vouch for you with stale, stagnant, cartelized, bureaucratized stamps of approval. In fact, you have no choice but to build a better signal.

More power is at your fingertips than ever before. The bad news, if you're lazy, is it won't be easy. You must want it. You must work for it. The good news is it's more rewarding, liberating, fun, effective, and engaging than the old crusty credentialist way.

Step out of the classroom. Step into the world. Discover and do what makes you come alive by trying stuff out. Build a body of work through skill and signal-building projects. Pitch your value to companies and customers with direct value propositions. Launch your career with the first, best real-world work you can get. Iterate, adapt, and create the career of your dreams. No degree required.

I'm not making this stuff up. My company, Praxis, has launched a few hundred careers in just this way. Young people with no degrees or experience have discovered their interests and abilities, built a profile of projects, and launched careers with a startup apprenticeship over and again. By the time their friends are stepping off campuses and shaking the mediocrity off their boots, these young Praxis participants are half a decade into a dynamic career making more money and having more fun than everyone around them.

Why not you?

NOTES

1. Louis L'Amour, *The Lonesome Gods* (New York: Bantam Books, 1983), 203.

"If you want to be financially-free, you need to become a different person than you are today and let go of whatever has held you back in the past."[1]

Robert Kiyosaki

THE ECONOMIC SECRETS OF GOING TO COLLEGE

by Dusty Wunderlich

It is your sophomore year of high school and you just started driving. You are experiencing a new kind of freedom for the first time. Adulthood is just around the corner, and your whole life is ahead of you. What a great time of life!

But there is a heaviness that is following you around. That heaviness comes in the form of a question: what are you going to do about college? Society is telling you this is the most important decision of your life, and you're feeling the weight of it.

Dusty Wunderlich is a fintech entrepreneur and economic theorist. Dusty's efforts are focused on research, advisory, and thought leadership for the next generation of financial technologies and economic models. Follow his work at dustywunderlich.com.

From the time you could remember, the adults around you have emphasized the importance of college. But what if someone told you it was ok to question college? The very freedom you have with that new driver's license is the same freedom you have over your choice of education and career. It probably sounds a bit rebellious to question college, but what if the facts supported you? Rather than just asking, "What college?" you should also be asking, "What if I did not go to college?"

Let's explore a few real-life stories to help explain the current economics of college and the job market. Instead of taking common knowledge at face value, we are going to explore what it really means to go to college today and let economics guide the way.

THE MILLION DOLLAR MAN

Thanks to student loans, more people can get a college degree than ever before. Many individuals are taking advantage of these loans and heading to college in the hopes of carving out a bright future.

In the late 1990s, Mike Meru was in high school asking the same questions most high school students ask themselves about college.[2] He, too, was probably excited about leaving home and experiencing the independence of college but nervous about the decision. Mike was fortunate; he was one of those individuals who knew exactly what he wanted to be when he grew up—an orthodontist.

Mike had issues with his teeth early in life and the hard work of orthodontists gave him the confidence he needed at a young age. Mike was so inspired by his experience that he wanted to do the same for others. He started to pursue his dream by completing his bachelor's degree at Brigham Young University. Mike was able to work during college and had the help of his parents to be able to finish his bachelor's degree debt free. Very few leave college with a bachelor's degree and no debt! This was an accomplishment in itself.

However, to be an orthodontist, Mike had to finish dental school and then do three more years of orthodontics school. Mike was not deterred by the challenge and set out on the next stage of his dream. Mike and his young family headed to California to attend the University of Southern California, one of the most prestigious dental schools in the country.

After finishing his fourth year in graduate school, Mike was $340,000 in debt with years to go until completion. There was doubt about whether he could afford to continue, but it was too late to turn back. Mike stayed the course, finished his schooling, and landed his dream job as an orthodontist in Draper, Utah, making $225,000 per year. Unfortunately, he had over $1,000,000 in student loans. Mike's monthly loan payment of $1,600 is not enough to cover the interest on that debt so the bill continues to grow. By the time he reaches retirement age, he will have paid over $2,000,000 on his debt.

The amount of Mike's student loans is rare, but his story is not. There are thousands of students who took on student debt to land their dream job who now find themselves in desperate situations. The American dream of being a college graduate has never been more attainable, but many are now questioning, "At what cost?"

THE BLUE COLLAR DROP OUT

Many millennials are starting to learn from stories like Mike Meru's and are bypassing college altogether to take blue-collar jobs.[3] They have seen those who came before get caught in the debt trap with no way out and have decided to opt-out altogether. Washington Mayancela is one of the individuals who decided to opt-out. Washington was in the top five in her class with a 4.0 GPA and plenty of opportunity and pressure to attend college. After living through the great recession, she didn't buy into the idea of the white-collar dream job and decided that blue-collar work was an admirable path she wanted to take.

At 18 years-old, Washington knew what the economics of college was all about. "Oh yes, the scholarships came in, but in the end my decision was more about economics and benefits and job satisfaction," she said. "I was 18 and it was a tough decision, but really I am glad I made it."

Washington started an apprenticeship as a pipefitter at 20-years old and has not looked back. When she completes her 5-year apprenticeship, she will earn $110 an hour as a steamfitter in New York City. No debt and $110 an hour is not a bad way to live. Washington is leading a group of intelligent high school students who are saying no to college and white-collar careers.

IVY LEAGUE BARTENDER

Nearly half of New York City-based millennials have student loans. Many of these college graduates are struggling to find their dream jobs or the dream job they have just isn't enough to make it in the Big Apple with student loans. The city of opportunity is not quite what it used to be. As a result, 1 out of every 2 millennials in New York is working in the restaurant industry to cover their student loans or basic living expenses.[4]

Even those we view as highly successful are not immune to the need to pick up a side gig bartending or waiting tables to make ends meet. The now nationally-recognized Congresswoman Alexandria Ocasio-Cortez was bartending in Union Square just a year before she was elected to Congress. Ocasio-Cortez graduated from the prestigious Boston University and still needed to work two jobs to provide for herself. She was fortunate to break through and get elected to Congress but many of her peers are still working two jobs to survive and pay off student loans.

These are just three of thousands of stories from across the country being lived by the next generation of students and workers. These examples illustrate that the decision to go to college has never been more complex and worthy of further exploration.

THE ECONOMICS OF COLLEGE

Most understand that supply and demand help set the prices for the items we purchase. The higher the supply of a product, the cheaper the price typically becomes. In reverse, if the supply decreases and there is high demand for the product, the price typically goes up. Since we live in a world with scarce resources, we use the price of items to help us to allocate those resources effectively.

At some point in your life, there was probably a hot product you wanted but could not get because the supply was limited or the price was higher than you could afford due to demand for the product. Supply and demand are the backbone of a market economy. The prices that emerge because of these principles allow entrepreneurs and consumers to give one another feedback about what consumers want more or less of.

The economic law of supply and demand also applies to services like education, but society does not like to frame education as a product or service. Yet, a college education is a product that consumers (i.e. students) are purchasing. It is important to remember that an individual's view of education does not change the mechanics of how students and consumers interact with education in an economic sense. This means the basic principles of supply and demand become vital to understanding the economics of college degrees.

Let's look back in time to when our grandparents or great-grandparents were young and deciding what to do after high school. In 1940, the Census Bureau started tracking levels of educational attainment. At that time, approximately 4.6 percent of the population had a four-year degree. Pursuing a four-year degree was a big deal back then because very few individuals chose that path. This created a very low supply of college graduates.

A lot has changed since 1940, but one of the most prominent changes in our society has been the supply of college graduates. Today, according to the census, approximately 32 percent of our population has a four-year degree or higher. Most look upon this as a great achievement and admire our highly educated society. There is certainly nothing wrong with learning and education, but too much of a good thing can have a negative effect.

This is where the story starts to get interesting. Let's go back in time again to learn more about our grandparents and great-grandparents. After World War II, many soldiers returned home and were able to take advantage of a free college education from the government through the GI Bill. This started the wave of higher education. There was still pent-up demand for college-educated workers in the economy at that point, and those returning from war who got a four-year degree were able to land high-paying, stable careers.

This taught an entire generation that higher education led to greater prosperity, and this belief was passed down to our parents and then to many of us in the younger generation. It was a simple equation: go to college and you will get a stable career.

As this wisdom was passed down to each generation, the laws of economics were ignored and college graduate supply started to grow exponentially. Eventually, the supply of college graduates surpassed the demand but for many, this was noticed too late. The turn of the century has brought great technological advancements but also two significant recessions. This is when the first weaknesses in the college graduate supply started to show. Recessions also result in unemployed workers returning to school for more education while the economy recovers, further inflating the supply of college-educated workers.

In 2013, reports started to surface that we were sending too many people to college. One of those reports stated that nearly half of college graduates were in jobs that did not require college degrees. Even worse, nearly 38 percent were jobs that did not require a high school diploma.[5] The world started to notice that something was awfully wrong with our perception of the need for higher education.

Unfortunately, these reports have done little to stop the problem, and college enrollments and the number of graduates continue to expand. The outlook is quite grim when the numbers are considered. The Census Bureau reported in 2018 that there are 50.4 million people in the country with a bachelor's degree. The yearly growth rate from 2015 to 2018 for students obtaining a bachelor's degree was 2.53 percent. At this rate, there will be approximately 62.7 million people with a bachelor's degree in 2026.

That sounds like a great statistic and one many would think is a great accomplishment for society. However, when viewed against the demand this tells a different story. The Bureau of Labor Statistics projects that approximately 3.3 million jobs will be created that require a bachelor's degree between 2016 to 2026. Based on that growth rate, the number of jobs requiring a degree will be 36.7 million.

Put simply, by 2026, there will be 62.7 million people with a college degree but only 36.7 million jobs that require one.

To no surprise, this oversupply of college graduates has created a shortage of skilled and semi-skilled blue-collar workers, and young people have taken notice. For example, the 10-year projected employment gain for carpenters nationwide is 24 percent with annual wages for experienced journeymen at nearly $90,000.[6] Our steam fitter Washington saw this trend and took advantage of this shortage; many more will follow her lead.

Our economy is like the engine in your car. It requires many unique parts working in unison to operate. Some parts are more expensive and have greater work capacity in the engine but even the smallest and least expensive part plays a crucial role in the operation of the engine. Likewise, there are many jobs that make our economy work efficiently. Pushing everyone along the same job path is the equivalent of trying to build a working engine with a pile of carburetors and spark plugs. It won't work, and this is why understanding the economic law of supply and demand is vital in understanding the economics of college degrees.

WHAT ABOUT PRICE?

Another important point to remember is that how much we value something also tends to decline when we accumulate more of the same product. This is another economic law that many intuitively know even if they know nothing about economics or business. The last section taught us that the supply of college graduates has gone up considerably in the last few decades, surpassing demand from employers. That would lead us to believe that this glut of graduates is due to the price of college decreasing—but is that really the case?

Unfortunately, the price of college continues to increase year-over-year and at a much faster pace than any other product or service. Since the late 1970s, the price of general goods has increased by approximately 250 percent. There are outliers like medical costs that have gone up nearly 600 percent but surpassing all goods and services by a long shot is college tuition, which has gone up over 1,100 percent in cost during that same time period.[7]

This tuition inflation is creating a significant problem and violates economic laws. We currently have an over-supply of college graduates, which means that the value of a college degree is continuing to decline every year. However, the price for a bachelor's degree continues to rise despite the decline in its value in the marketplace.

This economic anomaly is the very reason many high school graduates have started to surpass their college graduate counterparts in earning. In fact, a few years ago, high school graduates began to surpass college graduates in home ownership, credit scores, and auto ownership. This is a complete reversal from what college was intended to do, and had done, for many decades.[8]

Another important point to address is that the price of college does not differ according to the degree. Pricing is usually based on a credit hour and is not specific to the underlying course. Given that some degrees and courses have greater demand, or value, by employers, this makes it difficult to prioritize the degrees in certain areas that are in high demand over those that are in low demand.

This is the equivalent of a $5 grab bag that could have a diamond or a loaf of bread inside. You could get lucky and get a diamond and think that the grab bag is great, or you could end up with a bunch of stale bread. Pricing gives us valuable information to make sound decisions, and when pricing is absent or manipulated, it can lead people to make decisions they will later regret. Instead of each credit hour being $300, it would provide information for students about the value of certain degrees in the marketplace if an engineering course was $500 per credit hour and a hip-hop dance theory course was $100 per credit hour. Without objective prices, the students are buying grab bags and hoping they get the diamond.

The question remains, "What on earth would cause the price of a product to go up when the value of that product is declining?" And, "Why are college courses priced like a commodity?" We must look to student loans to understand why and how basic economic laws are being broken in the economics of college.

THE STUDENT LOAN MIRAGE

Understanding how we make decisions and choices about products and interest rates is crucial in understanding student loans. It's common to hear horror stories about people's inability to pay back their stu-

dent loans because of the interest rates. With a national student loan balance of $1.5 trillion, it has become
a reality that many have experienced for themselves
or second-hand through a friend.[9] Most of society is
scratching their heads on how we ended up here.

Making decisions about attending college is no different than deciding about buying a new car. Now that
college tuition is so expensive, most students must take
out student loans to afford it, just as most people borrow to purchase a car. Having to pay for a product over
time changes the complexity of the decision.

When we buy a car, the salesman comes to us with
a loan offer that breaks down the interest rate, monthly payment, and other terms of the loan. This gives us
valuable information about the decision that needs to
be made about purchasing a car. If the interest rate is
too high, we may be willing to stick with our current,
paid-off car a little longer to avoid taking out the loan.
But a low-interest rate and cheap monthly payment
could make the new car look quite attractive and make
us willing to sign the loan papers. The loan information
might also help us make the decision between buying
the Honda Civic or the Chevy Corvette. As you can
see, interest rates play a vital role in our decision-mak-
ing process.

In contrast, student loans have fixed interest rates and are available to almost anyone who wants to attend college. Unlike a car loan where the interest and terms of the loan vary according to the amount being borrowed and the lender's belief in the borrower's ability to pay, a loan with a fixed interest rate that is available to all does not give individuals an idea of how risky it is for them to agree to take out the loan for their college education. This has led thousands of people to make poor decisions about whether to go to college.

Let's go through a quick example: Susie and Jennifer were best friends since elementary school. In their senior year of high school, they were faced with the decision of choosing a college and potential major. Susie always liked the arts and showed great talent. Her parents told her she should follow her dream. She was thrilled to be accepted to Murray State University and decided to attend this prestigious school despite the cost, because she could take out student loans to cover it. Jennifer has always been drawn to math and the arts but is more risk-averse. She decided to attend the University of California, Berkeley for an engineering degree. Jennifer also needed to take out a student loan to cover tuition, housing, and supplies.

Fast forward 20 years and Jennifer and Susie meet up for dinner to talk about their lives. Susie has been in and out of jobs since graduating and currently works as a temporary executive assistant for a local business owner. She could not find full-time work as an artist, so takes whatever jobs she can do as she finds them. She has not paid off her student loans and often dreams about how different her life would have been had she not attended college. Jennifer, feeling guilty, downplays her current situation but she has excelled and is moving up the ranks of a regional engineering firm. She paid off her student loans five years after she graduated because engineering is a high-demand field and she was able to find a lucrative position right away.

During their dinner, Jennifer and Susie recognize their high school friend Bill at the table next to them. They have not seen him for 20 years, so he catches them up on his life. Bill was always the rebel at school and never really took to education. The decision for him to not attend college was easy. Instead, Bill became an apprentice to a plumber right out of high school and worked hard for ten years while saving every penny he could. After ten years, he launched his own plumbing business which employs 100 plumbers at ten locations in three different cities. Bill is personally debt-free and owns his home outright.

Statistically speaking, Jennifer's engineering degree from UC Berkley will make her $1.1 million more over a 20-year career than her peer with a high school diploma. Susie's art degree from Murray State will make her $150,000 less over a 20-year career than her peer with a high school diploma.[10]

This is the stark reality of college education and student loans. With an oversupply of college graduates, your choice of college and degree can have a huge effect on the rest of your life. Different careers have different levels of demand in the marketplace, making some majors dramatically more profitable than others. Unfortunately, fixed interest rates on student loans do not give students any information on how to choose a degree that will provide a worthwhile income. Susie had to learn this the hard way, and it's a decision that will haunt her for life.

We are willing to delay our gratification if the result is more rewarding in the long term. That is the essence of the decision we make about whether to go to college. We are delaying the gratification of gainful employment and wages now for the prospect of better employment and wages in the future. But, with nearly 50 percent of college graduates in careers that do not require a college degree, these individuals delayed instant gratification and made an investment that resulted in *worsening* their situation compared to what they could have obtained in the present moment.

In an ideal world, Susie's student loan application would have been denied or the interest rate would have been much higher to reflect the lender's understanding that full-time jobs related to art are rare and often don't pay well. It is, therefore, riskier for them to lend to people pursuing an art degree, so the terms of the loan would reflect that reality. This would have given Susie the valuable information she needed to make the decision about college and her degree. She may have still chosen to take the loan, but she would have known to have a backup plan in place, maybe to double major in a more lucrative field. Without the information the terms of a loan provide student borrowers, future students rarely have any idea of the inherent risks they are making that can impact their life for years to come. They can only discover this information for themselves through personal research that is often hard to come by in our college-obsessed society.

A PRODUCT YOU CAN'T RETURN

I bought a new blender from Amazon that was recommended to me by a friend. It was supposed to be the latest and greatest blender on the market. I did the one-button buy and it was on my front porch in two days. I was anxious to get it out of the box and give it a try.

To say I was disappointed in the product would be an understatement. It did not perform at all like it was advertised. The next day, I hit the return button, shipped it back to Amazon, and was given a full refund.

This process happens thousands of times a day throughout the economy. Consumers and companies are constantly buying and returning products for many reasons. This is typically done cordially and voluntarily. We are so used to returning something that is broken or did not perform as advertised that we don't even question this process.

Except when it comes to education! Have you ever heard of an individual returning their college degree after they entered the job market and found out it didn't help them find a job? Probably not—because it does not happen. Education is probably the most expensive product that you will ever buy that you cannot return if it doesn't work. Considering half of the college graduates in the market are not using their degree, I would think they would love the option to return the product and get their money back.

This often gets overlooked in education, but it tells us a lot about college economics. Imagine if you could build a product that went up in price every year and could never be returned? Would that not make you think differently about how you produced and advertised your product?

Colleges are not incentivized to make sure students land a lucrative career or even use their degree. They are incentivized by students enrolling and taking classes. Whether those classes lead to a job or not is irrelevant from their perspective. If colleges were held accountable for how many of their students obtained a job in their field of study, it would trigger an entire overhaul of how the college system works.

This lack of product accountability is the primary reason that colleges are not trying to match the supply of degrees (i.e. graduates) to the demand of the labor markets. This is also why college credit hours are priced like a commodity and not priced dynamically based on demand. Given that the current model is working quite well for colleges, it's probably not likely to change anytime soon. However, it is important that future students know that they are buying a product that cannot be returned and might not actually work as advertised. Remember, when it comes to college, all sales are final. Buyer beware!

SHOULD COLLEGE BE "FREE"?

There are many advocates who study the economics of college degrees who think the solution is free college for everyone. That sure sounds nice but the idea is too good to be true.

The vast majority of the jobs in our economy do not require a college degree, so allowing everyone to go to college would have many adverse results. It would take valuable workers who are currently working in our economy out of the workforce. This would ultimately drive down economic output and tax revenue that would be needed to fund free college. (Those college professors must be paid somehow.)

A larger problem is that when we do not put an objective price on a product, it can lead to poor decision making. Prices allow us to value and rank products and services. This economic calculation is vital in making sure we are allocating our resources efficiently and appropriately. Without a price for college, many individuals would gravitate toward their passions or away from their current jobs that do not require a college degree. This sounds great in theory, but it might not line up with the reality of what jobs need to be performed. We have already learned from prior examples that this leads to many bad outcomes. An individual might get a degree in a field they are passionate about, but that does not mean that degree is marketable.

The economy is not absorbing the current supply of college graduates; making college free would only exacerbate this issue. Before you jump on the free college bandwagon, it's important to think through the economics of college and how this will likely make you worse off in the long term.

WHAT TO DO NOW?

Now that you are an expert on the economics of college, the question remains, what to do now? Below are a few things to consider as you approach the question of "what if?"

Calculate your Return on Investment

A college education must be viewed as an investment, and any rational businessperson wants to know what their return on investment is likely to be before they invest. Students must make the same calculation when deciding what college to attend, if at all.

Thankfully, we live in the Internet age and have access to many great resources and data. Companies like Payscale give return-on-investment predictions for nearly every university and degree. This allows students to understand the financial risk of the school or degree they are considering.

Some individuals might review the analysis and decide college is not worth the investment at all, and that is a perfectly fine conclusion. Don't fall for the "follow your dream" speech now that you know the potential consequences that could lead to a nightmare. Be an astute investor by doing your homework before you make the investment.

Don't Go into Debt

Although college tuition continues to rise significantly each year, there are still ways you can get through college debt-free should you choose to attend. Going into a college education with the goal of taking on no debt will change your perspective and approach.

For example, you could go to your local community college to obtain an associate degree. Community colleges typically cater to non-traditional students who have families or full-time jobs. This will give you the opportunity to work while attending college. And know this: the credits you earn from a community college don't change the final bachelor's degree you get from your desired four-year institution. You basically get the same degree at a discount. If you're going to go shopping for a degree, why not bargain shop?

Once you do decide to transfer to a four-year college, make sure to do the research and pick the university that will give you the best bang for your buck. Take advantage of scholarships and in-state tuition to reduce costs. You might not attend the prestigious university you wanted, but no piece of paper or experience is worth being in debt for 20 years.

Work for a Start-Up

If you realize that the economics of college just don't make sense and you want to be a rebel, then you will be in good company with many other start-up entrepreneurs who have recognized some of the problems and chosen an alternative path. Over the past 20 years, an entirely new business culture has emerged in the form of technology start-up companies. These trail-blazing entrepreneurs are pushing back on the status quo. They are bypassing individuals with years of experience and fancy degrees for young and talented individuals looking to work hard and learn on the job.

Working for a start-up is a great way to learn and gain experience at a fast pace. It can mean hard work and little pay at times but can also be very rewarding. Getting that first professional work experience is always the most important step. Working for a start-up allows for that experience and will allow you to develop the skills needed to work for more established companies in the future. All without college and student loans.

Consider a Different Form of Higher Education

The cost of a college education is starting to drive entrepreneurs to create affordable education products. There is a significant shortage of workers in certain areas of the economy, including software developers. Coding academies and schools are starting to emerge to train new computer developers in as little as 6-months. Even better, some are guaranteeing job placements and certain levels of starting salaries, or you get your money back. Imagine that: an education product you can actually get your money back for if it does not work as promised.

This is not just for coding. There are many trade schools and academies that are adapting to the fast-paced economy. These education and training products are about efficiency and adaptability to industry. They allow individuals to quickly learn what is relevant in the market. Four-year colleges are starting to lose pace to these more adaptive schools, which is why this is a good option for those looking for some education outside of high school but aren't willing to go the traditional college route.

It is more important than ever to understand the economics of a college degree and that it's perfectly fine—and logical—to question going to college. The laws of economics require us to question the current state of college. Education is always worthwhile, but an education is not confined to college campuses or a bachelor's degree.

NOTES

1. Robert Kiyosaki, "Define Financial Freedom," Rich Dad, accessed May 9, 2019, https://www.richdad.com/resources/define-financial-freedom.

2. Josh Mitchell, "Mike Meru Has $1 Million in Student Loans. How Did That Happen?," *The Wall Street Journal*, May 25, 2018, https://www.wsj.com/articles/mike-meru-has-1-million-in-student-loans-how-did-that-happen-1527252975.

3. John Aidan Byrne, "Why Millennials are Forgoing College for Blue-Collar Jobs," *The New York Post*, July 31, 2016, https://nypost.com/2016/07/31/why-millennials-are-forgoing-college-for-blue-collar-jobs/.

4. John Aidan Byrne, "New York's Millennials are Waiting Tables to Pay Off Student Loans," *The New York Post*, February 2, 2019, https://nypost.com/2019/02/02/new-yorks-millennials-are-waiting-tables-to-pay-off-student-loans/.

5. Susan Adams, "Half Of College Grads Are Working Jobs That Don't Require A Degree," *Forbes*, May 28, 2013, https://www.forbes.com/sites/susan-adams/2013/05/28/half-of-college-grads-are-working-jobs-that-dont-require-a-degree/#1a4b577b6d7a.

6. U.S. Department of Labor salary data analysis.

7. Consumer Price Index data analysis.

8. . Meta Brown, "Young Student Loan Borrowers Retreat from Housing and Auto Markets," Liberty Street Economics, Federal Reserve Bank of New York, April 17, 2013, https://libertystreeteconomics.newyorkfed.org/2013/04/young-student-loan-borrowers-retreat-from-housing-and-auto-markets.html.

9. Federal Reserve data.

10. "Is College Worth It?," *The Economist*, April 5, 2014, https://www.economist.com/united-states/2014/04/05/is-college-worth-it.

"The difference between great people and everyone else is that great people create their lives actively, while everyone else is created by their lives, passively waiting to see where life takes them next. The difference between the two is the difference between living fully and just existing."[1]

Michael E. Gerber

MORE THAN JUST A JOB

HOW TO BUILD YOUR BRAND

by Josh Steimle

I'm not anti-college. I loved college. I plan to return to school for doctoral work and to become a research professor. My perspective on higher education is that while it's necessary for some and helpful for others, many individuals could achieve similar results faster, better, and more cheaply through other means.

There are four primary benefits of attending college:

1. **Productivity gains.** Those who obtain a college education gain knowledge and skills that make

---

Josh Steimle is an entrepreneur who has built multiple six and seven-figure businesses. He is an author, TEDx speaker (see his talk on homeschooling on YouTube), and has been featured in dozens of publications including *Forbes*, *Fortune*, *TIME*, and *Entrepreneur*.

them more valuable in the workplace and are therefore able to demand higher compensation.

2. **Structural requirements.** Many higher paying positions require a college degree as a matter of policy. Having a relevant degree allows access to certain fields. As presently arranged in our society, it is virtually impossible to become a doctor, lawyer, or teacher without first obtaining the necessary degree.

3. **Network benefits.** Attending college results in beneficial friendships and associations that can lead to better job and business opportunities. It's "who you know, more than what you know," some would say.

4. **Brand value.** A student graduating in 2018 with an MBA from Harvard Business School could expect a starting salary of over $160,000. While the quality of the education is certainly a factor, does anyone doubt the value of the Harvard brand?

There are also non-economic reasons one might attend college. I met my wife at college and made many treasured friends. However, since one could make the case that rewarding relationships and life experiences can happen outside of college, I will restrict my comments to the economic side of the question.

When it comes to deciding whether to go to college or not, the question to answer is not whether college is beneficial as it would be difficult to find someone who has not benefited in some way from their college experience. The real debate is whether college is worth the cost, especially when there are other options available to obtain similar benefits.

As the cost of a degree increases, so does the incentive to find alternative means of achieving the results a degree provides. According to a 2016 study by the National Center for Education Statistics (NCES), an arm of the U.S. Department of Education, only sixty percent of full-time undergraduate students earn a four-year degree within six years of starting. Six years is a long time, no matter how old you are. If you're sixty, that's ten percent of your life. It's an eternity when you're twenty.

NCES also calculated the average annual cost of an undergraduate education to be $16,757 at public universities, $43,065 at private nonprofit colleges, and $23,776 at private for-profit institutions. Those costs were up thirty-four percent at public institutions in 2016 compared to ten years before, and up twenty-six percent at private nonprofit institutions, after adjusting for inflation.

That lowest cost of $17,000 per year is still a lot of money. Even someday when you're making six figures you'll still say "Did I really spend that much per year on college? That's nuts."

Six years of full-time studying, at a cost between $100,000 and $260,000? For most of us, the math doesn't compute. According to the Bureau of Labor Statistics' (BLS) 2016 Consumer Expenditure Survey, the average American earns $74,664 in annual pretax income, and after subtracting all necessary expenses, not including payments on student loan debt, we find there's $6,863 left over. Assuming one's entire education was financed with student loans, and if 100% of one's discretionary income was dedicated to paying off those loans, it would take the average American somewhere between 14 to 38 years to pay them off.

Both in terms of both time and money, college is expensive.

As a prospective student, you may hear stories about recent graduates who struggle to find a job while battling mountains of debt. It may make you wonder if you're on the path to a happy, successful life. Are years of debt payments the best you can expect?

You may live as frugally as possible, but unless someone else is paying for your education, it's somewhere between difficult and impossible to pay your way through college and graduate without debt. It didn't use to be this way, but today the system is stacked against you. The good news is there are ways to beat the system. There are ways to receive most of the benefits you would get from college, without ever going. I know because most of what I've achieved professionally was not the result of my college education.

I have a master's degree in information systems management. However, I started a business while in college that is unrelated to my major. I might as well have not had a college education for all it did for me as an entrepreneur. What success I've achieved was assisted by mentors, good books, and experience. And one other thing: personal branding.

WHAT'S A PERSONAL BRAND?

According to Jeff Bezos, "Your brand is what others say about you when you're not in the room."

What do people say about *you*? Do they say, "She's super techie. She knows how to fix anything in a computer," or "He's a marketing expert. If it's anything to do with marketing, he's your guy."

You already have a personal brand, but is it the personal brand you want? Is it as powerful as you'd like it to be?

For the past several years I've studied the personal brands of highly influential people to find out what they did to build such powerful personal brands. I found there are seven primary "systems" they use. Chances are you are also using some of these systems to some degree, although you may not know it. By coming to know and understand each system and applying them intentionally, you will create a powerful personal brand and wield exceptional influence—no degree required. I know you can do it because I did it.

HOW I ENDED UP ON A DESERT ISLAND WITH RICHARD BRANSON

I started my business in 1999 while I was a college student. The business, MWI, is a digital marketing agency, and it's still running today.

MWI has had plenty of ups and downs. The dotcom crash in 2000 almost put us under. Then came 9/11. Worst of all, while we did a good job at marketing our clients, we never seemed to have the time or resources for our own marketing.

That all changed in 2013 when I brought on Corey Blake as a partner, which freed up a significant part of my time, and I had the opportunity to write for Forbes. Writing for Forbes opened doors for me to write for other outlets, and I eventually wrote over 300 articles for over twenty publications, such as Fortune, Time, Entrepreneur, Inc., Mashable, and TechCrunch. My writing led to a book deal, a TEDx talk, and speaking engagements around the world. Most importantly, it generated attention for MWI and led to a steady stream of clients and millions of dollars in revenue that allowed us to open offices in Asia, Europe, and the US.

In late 2016 my book caught the eye of someone planning a gathering of marketing executives in the Caribbean on Necker Island, owned by Richard Branson. All expenses were covered, and I spent a week with an amazing group of leading marketers, including Branson himself.

At no point was my degree a factor in my success. MWI's clients have never asked about my degree, except in casual conversation. None of the publications I've written for has brought it up. Branson did not require my transcripts before allowing me on his island.

But my personal brand? None of my current success could have happened without it.

It was only when I invested seriously in my personal brand, starting in 2013 when I began writing for Forbes, that I was able to land larger clients, open offices around the world, and generate millions in revenue for my business. Many other entrepreneurs have used their personal brands to build their businesses as I have done, and on a much grander scale. You don't need to be an entrepreneur to benefit from a personal brand. Your personal brand can benefit you as a working professional, teacher, parent, spouse, friend, writer, or artist.

In this chapter, I'll show you how to build your own personal brand using a framework I created called The 7 Systems of Influence. If you do not yet have a college degree, once you learn the power of building a personal brand, you may wonder whether you need to go to college at all.

THE 7 SYSTEMS OF INFLUENCE

System 1: Vision

Many invest time and money to build personal brands, and they don't even know why they're doing it. As Stephen R. Covey once wrote:

People are working harder than ever, but because they lack clarity and vision, they aren't getting very far. They, in essence, are pushing a rope with all of their might.[2]

Covey wrote a book you may have heard of called *The 7 Habits of Highly Successful People.* In it, Covey teaches his readers to "begin with the end in mind." What plane ever reached its destination without the pilot knowing where he wanted to go? Yet executives do this all the time with their personal brands. They believe if they build it, the benefits will come. That kind of thinking may work in the movies, but in real life not so much.

"I'd like to do some speaking gigs, maybe write a book," an executive says.

Fine, but *why*? What's the point?

Getting paid to speak, landing a book deal, growing a huge following on LinkedIn, being featured in top business publication—these are means to an end, not the end itself. The first step to building a powerful personal brand is to have a clearly defined, long-term objective, a vision of the future.

When I started my agency, my dream was to build the largest digital marketing agency in the world. That is still my dream. But between 1999, when I started the company, and 2013, that dream didn't get very far. Even when I began to write for Forbes, I didn't experience immediate success. I wrote a lot of articles, but they weren't focused on any particular topic. I wrote articles about what it was like to be an entrepreneur, politics, how Jay-Z's app-based album launch had gone wrong—anything that seemed interesting that I had an opinion about.

Then I started writing about digital marketing. I wrote from my substantial experience working with hundreds of clients and gave away all my secrets and best advice for free in my articles. Soon my agency was flooded with leads from people who read my articles and wanted to work with us.

What's your vision? What do you want to accomplish? What impact do you want to make in the world?

System 2: Genius Zone

Each of us has a unique combination of skills, abilities, and experiences. In his book *The Big Leap*, author Gay Hendricks talks about "expert zones" and your "genius zone." Just because you're good at something, the skills in your expert zone, doesn't mean you should do it. When you focus on your genius zone, the areas where you are truly unique, you will be able to do things nobody else can. We often get sucked into spending time on our expert zones and miss out on our zone of true genius.

While your genius zone may be related to innate talents and abilities you possess, you don't need to feel pigeonholed. You can choose what you want your genius zone to be. As Al Ries and Jack Trout wrote in their book *Positioning*, "What position do you want to occupy in your audience's mind?"[3]

System 2 helps you identify your expert zones and use them to find your genius zone. Begin by creating a long list of all your expert zones. For example, I've run a marketing agency for 20 years, so marketing is definitely one of my expert zones. I've also lived in China, so compared to someone who has never lived in China, I could be called an expert. Note that you don't need to be The Best or The Most Knowledgeable at something in order to be an expert. Here's an abbreviated list of my expert zones:

- Marketing
- China
- Brazil
- Skateboarding
- Politics
- Economics
- Entrepreneurship
- Sales
- Thought leadership

- LinkedIn
- Writing
- Public speaking
- Podcasting
- Email list building
- Online course building
- Parenting

What are your expert zones? List everything you can think of, even if it seems very basic. For example, having grown up in the US I know a lot more about the US than I do about China and Brazil, and yet it might not occur to me to list that I'm an expert on the US because I'm surrounded by others who are just as experienced as I am. However, compared to someone who grew up in China and has never been to the US, your level of expertise is off the charts. If you're 15 years old, you might not feel like an expert at much, but compared to a 70-year-old, you are an expert at what it's like to be a 15 year old today, and some 15-year-olds have leveraged this expertise to become consultants to Fortune 500 companies trying to figure out how to sell to today's teens.

Next, we overlap our expert zones to find potential genius zones, like this:

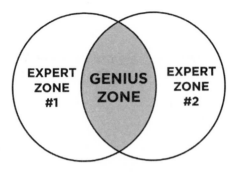

For example, although I know a lot about marketing, that doesn't make me unique by itself because a lot of other people know just as much or more about marketing.

I also know a lot about skateboarding. I've been involved in the skateboarding industry for decades, but that doesn't make me unique because there are 20 million other skateboarders in the world. However, how many people know as much about marketing *and* skateboarding as I do? Maybe a dozen. Skateboarding plus marketing could be my genius zone.

While skateboarding plus marketing isn't the intersection I've chosen to make my genius zone, this example shows how experimenting with overlapping interests will help you find a niche around which to build a powerful personal brand.

System 3: Audience

You now have a clear vision of your future and what makes you uniquely suited to make that future a reality. The next question is, who do you need to influence in order to achieve your vision?

Just as you used your expert zones to find your genius zone, you can use a list of potential audiences to find your ideal audience.

As you create your list, the quickest way to find your ideal audience is to focus on those with the following characteristics:

- **Are like you.** All other things being equal, you'll find it easier to connect and relate to people who are like you, and people who are like you will also connect more quickly to you.
- **Want what you are selling.** If you're selling marketing services, then target people who want to buy marketing services. Sounds like common sense, but it's funny how often we get simple things like this wrong. When considering a potential audience, don't just ask "does this type of person ever buy what I'm selling?" because the answer will almost always be "yes, sometimes they do." Instead ask, "Is what I'm selling a must-have for this person?"

- **Can afford to buy what you're selling.** People who want what you have and those who will buy it are two separate groups. College students may want to buy a $5,000 per month life coaching service, but perhaps successful executives with a $10 million net worth are an easier sell.
- **Energize you.** If you spent a day speaking to your audience at an event or writing a book for them, would you be drained at the end of the day and never want to do it again, or would you wake up the next morning excited to do it all over again? If working with your audience drains you, it may be that you're not working with them the right way (see System 4: Content) but it also may be you've chosen the wrong audience to focus on.

Brainstorm a list of all your potential audiences. Even if you're pretty sure they're not going to be your ideal audience, list them out anyway to make sure you're not missing anyone. For example, one of my recent client's lists included:

- Females
- Entrepreneurs
- Startups
- Friends
- Business associates

- Children
- Parents
- Students
- Poor people
- Leukemia—children and families
- Singaporean
- Global

Now, begin to overlap your audiences. In the case of my client, she overlapped several potential audiences to reach the conclusion that her ideal audience is successful, female, Asian entrepreneurs who want to expand their businesses to China. This is exactly who she is, as well, with the one difference being that she already has experience expanding businesses into China, so she is in a great position to help her ideal audience do the same.

System 4: Content

As I talk about creating content, you might say, "But I wasn't trained as a writer," or "I'm not a video expert." I also didn't go to journalism or writing school, yet I've written hundreds of articles for some of the best-known publications in the world. I don't consider myself a video expert, yet I've made videos that have gone viral and been seen hundreds of thousands of times. You don't need to be an expert at creating content to make something that will establish you as an expert.

In addition, we need to redefine what "content" is. Your content is more than a blog post, a book, or a video. It's *everything* you do. It's your example, your actions, or lack thereof. If you wake up early every day and work out, and tell your friend about your morning routine, that's content. If you abstain from alcohol at business events, people will notice, and that's content. If you write in your journal, that's content as well. You are a content machine! Now let's put that machine to use to create the impact you want to have on the world.

The first step to creating compelling content is to decide what your message will be. Once you have that message, every piece of content you consciously create for your ideal audience will reinforce that message.

During WWII, Churchill's message to his audience, the British people, was "we are going to win." Gandhi's message to the people of India, as well as the British people, was "we deserve to be free." Mother Teresa's message was "one person can make a difference."

Bringing it a little closer to earth, Gary Vaynerchuk's message is "if you're a young entrepreneur, here's how to be successful." Amy Porterfield's is "if you're an entrepreneur, I will teach you how to build email lists and create online courses." For Ramit Sethi, it's "if you're a millennial, I will teach you how to manage your finances and become rich."

As you think about your own message for your ideal audience, bear in mind your message will be more effective if it is:

1. **Customer-centric.** It's not about you; it's about your customer. Your customer is the hero in this story, and you are the guide.
2. **Must-have.** You solve a problem. What makes the result you deliver a must-have for your audience?
3. **Wrapped in a story.** We evolved to pay attention to stories. Stories will capture your audience's attention.
4. **Credible.** How can you make your message more credible? In a court of law, credibility comes from evidence and witnesses. What evidence and witnesses can you produce to back up your message?
5. **Individualized.** The most effective message is delivered in person, one-on-one. It may not always, or ever, be possible for you to deliver your message that way, but how can you get as close as possible?

We're not done with content yet! You now have your message, but how are you going to deliver it to your audience?

What's your channel?

The place where you deliver your message is your channel. Ten-thousand years ago, cavemen painted on the cave wall as their channel. Today you can write a book, article, or social media post, speak on a podcast or on the stage, film a video for YouTube, or choose from a hundred other channels. While the act of creating a message and delivering it to your audience is fundamental marketing and never changes, the channels are changing every day.

While you can target multiple channels, you have limited time, and it's likely that one channel will deliver the bulk of your results. It's also important to take into account which channel best matches your talents. When deciding what your primary channel should be, answer these two questions:

1. Where does your audience hang out where they're open to receiving a message like yours?
2. How do you prefer to communicate with your audience? Are you a better writer than you are a speaker, or prefer another way to create content?

Is there a channel that jumps out as being the obvious choice? If not, talk to members of your ideal audience to get their opinions.

How do you create compelling content?

Many books have been written about how to create great content, so I'll only provide a few high-level observations.

First, just do it. Your first attempts at creating content are likely to fall flat. You'll do things wrong. You'll make mistakes. It's ok, everyone does. This quote from Reid Hoffman, founder of LinkedIn, holds true as well for content as it does for building products:

> If you are not embarrassed by the first version of your product, you've launched too late.[4]

Second, keep it simple. If you make things complicated, you'll never get started. That's where the next system comes in.

System 5: Action

I will say this about college: it gives you a deadline and an easy way to know if you're making progress. However, you can do that for yourself, for free, and save a few years and a few hundred thousand dollars. All it takes is minimal self-discipline and a good plan.

Benjamin Franklin is credited with saying "If you fail to plan, you plan to fail." We all know someone who says they're going to write that book...someday. They're going to give a TEDx talk...someday. They're going to make a difference in the world...someday.

Maybe that person is you.

I know how it goes because I've been there. Every highly influential person has been there. Perhaps the only difference between highly influential people and you is that they've failed more times than you've tried.

A lot of bright, intelligent people who are capable of becoming highly influential get through the first four Systems of Influence and then stop. As a result, their message doesn't reach their audience, nobody knows they exist, and nothing happens. Their vision never becomes reality.

Highly influential people have an Action System that makes it easy for them to create compelling content strategically and regularly. They have a system for writing a book every year, speaking at 50 events, or posting daily on social media.

Sound overwhelming? Don't worry about it, if you start with small, simple steps, you'll be amazed at how far they take you. As Jeff Goins said:

The idea of writing a 500-page masterpiece can be paralyzing. Instead, write a short book of poems or stories. Long projects are daunting. Start small.[5]

There are a lot of ways to get started, the important thing is that your Action System works for you. It can be a project management tool or a piece of paper. Regardless, I recommend you:

1. **Start small.** What's the smallest step you can take to create content so you can test things out and see how your audience reacts? Maybe it's something quick on Twitter. Maybe it's a short post on LinkedIn. Maybe it's writing a one-page description of your book and emailing it to a few members of your audience. Maybe it's the first iteration of your email newsletter. Make it small, something you can complete today, or even within the next hour.

2. **Analyze.** How will you measure success? Set standards so you know whether your content is having the desired effect or not. These need not be complicated, the simpler the better.

3. **Repeat.** Once you complete your analysis, incorporate the feedback you've received, and create a second piece of content.

If you're not sure where to start, follow the advice from Marcus Sheridan in his book *They Ask, You Answer* and answer the questions your audience has. If your channel is LinkedIn, and you don't know what to post there, create a post and ask your connections to comment with questions they have about your genius zone. Now you've already created your first post, and you've got material to create several more. Create a post for each question and give your answer. Done. Easy.

You might also do as Gary Vaynerchuk recommends and "document, don't create." Create content about your vision, and then document the process of getting there.

System 6: Collaboration

Highly influential people never work alone.

My friend Derek Andersen created Startup Grind as a series of monthly fireside chats focused on entrepreneurship. At each event, he interviewed a different successful entrepreneur. At first, a handful of people attended the meetups, but then Derek invited others to start local chapters of Startup Grind and host their own events. There are now over 500 chapters of Startup Grind worldwide, and over 1.5 million people have attended Startup Grind events. Derek could never have made this impact on his own.

Harper Lee, whose book, *To Kill a Mockingbird*, seems like the perfect example of a highly influential person who didn't collaborate, was friends with Truman Capote and was influenced and aided by him. In addition, she never would have written her famous book if two of her friends hadn't gifted her a year's salary so she could take time off to write it. As Helen Keller once wrote, "Alone we can do so little; together we can do so much."[6]

Who can you collaborate with? Who do you share your genius zone with? Who else is targeting your ideal audience? Can you turn your ideal audience into collaborators who spread your message?

As with every other system, it's often best to start out small and test your ideas before launching into a huge project. Before you try to set up a website or other method to collaborate with thousands of people, try collaborating with one person manually to see what issues come up and how you can find the best win-win situation possible.

System 7: Love

"Great, way to make it awkward."

Don't worry, I'm not talking about that kind of love.

The Greeks had four different words for what they saw as four different kinds of love. *Storge* was love for one's family or kin, *philia* was the love you have for a friend, *eros* was sexual and romantic love, and divine love was *agape*.

When we say, "I like you as a friend, but..." what we're really saying is "I feel philia for you, but not eros."

When it comes to The 7 Systems of Influence, the kind of love we talk about is also most definitely not eros. Sorry, it's not you; it's me.

The love we're talking about is also not exactly agape, nor storge or philia, although it overlaps with those three. It's also not the "unconditional positive regard" sometimes mentioned by psychologists. Perhaps the easiest way to describe the kind of love highly influential people on LinkedIn have, the kind of love you want to also have, is to show how it applies in three other areas we already discussed:

1. Vision
2. Audience
3. Collaborators

Love for Your Vision. When you love your vision, it shows. This love can best be described as enthusiasm, passion, excitement, or keen interest. It's a key component of authenticity because we can sense when someone has a clear idea of what they want to accomplish and that they're pursuing it with intensity. That kind of intense interest breeds trust.

For example, imagine you started a shoe company for trail runners, but you're not a trail runner. In fact, you're not interested in trails, running, shoes, or fitness generally. What you're interested in is starting a successful business that will be highly profitable, and you did some analysis and found that this is a market niche where you can make a lot of money.

It's not a bad thing to want to own a successful company that makes good money, but what if someone comes along who has all the business skills you do, but is also an avid trail runner? This person loves getting out on the trails, running in races, and talking about trail running. Who is going to be committed to this business when times get tough? Who is going to see it through, no matter what? Who is going to pour everything she has into it? If you weren't an entrepreneur, but an outside investor, who would you rather invest in?

Is your vision a means to an end, or something you love, something you're passionate about, in and of itself?

Love for Your Audience. Remember when we talked above about finding your ideal audience? I said that one of the ways you know you've found your ideal audience is because they energize you. That's part of loving your audience, but it's not enough.

In his book, *The 7 Habits of Highly Effective People*, Covey said that love is a verb. If love were only a feeling, we'd constantly be confused about who we love because there is no one who energizes us 100% of the time. Even when we've found our ideal audience, we'll sometimes get drained and need a break. If you ever feel this way, that doesn't mean you chose the wrong audience. It might mean you need to serve them better.

When my first child, a daughter, was born, I expected that I would hold her for the first time and this amazing feeling would come over me and there would be an instant bond. Instead, I felt nothing. I mean, she was cute and everything, but no more than any other baby. Was something wrong with me? I wasn't sure, and I was afraid to talk about it with anyone.

Over the next several weeks I did what new dads do. I changed her diaper, bathed her, held her, and talked to her. In short, I served her. As the weeks passed, I noticed my feelings change. I started to feel a special affection for my daughter, and the more I invested time in serving her, the more that love grew.

Excitement, logic, and reason might help you find your ideal audience, but if you're struggling to feel that excitement, try serving more deeply. You might find that love for your audience is not something magical that appears out of nowhere, but rather the tangible result of the service you provide to them.

Love for Your Collaborators. When you are filled with love, collaborators will flock to you. People love to work with people who are passionate about what they do. Perhaps there is an evolutionary component to this. It's not difficult to imagine that someone who loves what he does is more likely to be successful at it than another person who does it out of mere necessity. Which caveman would be more likely to survive: the one who sees hunting as a pleasurable art form that contributes to the health and happiness of his family and clan or the one who sees hunting as necessary for survival and thinks his clan is a burden? Which type of caveman would you rather have in your clan?

When you are passionate about your vision and love your audience, it's magnetic, it's inspiring, and partners will want to work with you. They'll want to work with you, not just because it's more exciting, but because they sense the likelihood of success.

I was once talking with a friend of mine about our parents and his rough upbringing, and he said, "You know, your dad can do a lot of things wrong, but if you know he loves you, it covers up a lot of mistakes."

If your heart is in the right place, you don't have to execute everything else in these lessons perfectly. In fact, you can make a lot of mistakes. Yet, if you truly care, your audience will forgive you.

CONCLUSION

The idea that everyone should get a college degree is recent and likely to be short-lived. Not much more than 100 years ago, only 4% of young people in the United States attended college. During the 1900s government funding poured into higher education through public universities and subsidies like the GI bill, Pell Grants, and federally guaranteed student loans. Easy money created artificial demand and a higher education bubble, especially since the 1980s. Since the main source of funding for both public and private universities was the government, rather than focusing on students or the businesses that would employ them, schools focused their efforts on complying with government-mandated accreditation programs and politically correct curriculum. This caused a disconnect between much of what students are taught in college and what employers are seeking. Where there is less of a disconnect between what students receive and what employers require it is, regrettably, due to government licensing programs that force employers in certain fields to require college degrees.

Andrew Carnegie, who escaped poverty and starvation in his native Scotland to eventually become a successful entrepreneur and the richest man in America, presciently stated in 1901 that "a college education unfits rather than fits men to affairs."[7]

This disparity between what the world needs, and what universities are providing, can last for only so long. As the price of a college degree rises, employers demand more applicable skills, and a college education (if not the degree) is increasingly available for free online, a diploma will be seen as an arbitrary and unnecessary requirement.

Perhaps you are wondering why, given what I've said here, I plan to return to school for five years to get a Ph.D. and then be a university professor. In part, it's because the degree, the knowledge, the enhancement to my personal brand, and the network I'll gain from going back to school will help me achieve my vision in ways I couldn't accomplish without them. If there were a cheaper, faster, better way to achieve my vision, I'd take that route, but after 10 years of researching other options, I haven't found a better one.

You may be in similar circumstances. Perhaps you want to become a doctor and cure cancer. Sure, you could educate yourself without college and medical school, and even possibly become more knowledgeable and experienced than most cancer specialists. But the medical community and society at large would reject you, and you would constantly be fighting to have your work taken seriously. Can you do more good outside the system or within it? Some battles are worth fighting, some aren't.

Then again, if your vision is to cure cancer, but not necessarily become a doctor, consider that the late Jon Huntsman, a successful businessman, donated $1.4 billion of his fortune to cure cancer and inspired others to donate several hundred million more. Is that route more to your liking? Then perhaps skipping college, obtaining an education on your own, and building a personal brand might be your fastest path to making your dreams a reality.

NOTES

1. Michael E. Gerber, *The E-Myth Revisited: Why Most Small Businesses Don't Work and What to Do About It* (New York: HaperCollins, 1995), 139.
2. Stephen R. Covey, *The 8th Habit: From Effectiveness to Greatness* (New York: Free Press, 2004), 218.
3. Al Ries and Jack Trout, *Positioning: The Battle for Your Mind* (New York: McGraw-Hill, 2001).
4. Reid Hoffman, Twitter, accessed May 8, 2019, https://twitter.com/reidhoffman/status/847142924240379904.
5. Jeff Goins, "10 Bonus Tips for Writing a Book," Goins, Writer, accessed May 8, 2019, https://goinswriter.com/writing-tips-bonus/.
6. Dorothy Herrmann, *Helen Keller: A Life* (Chicago: The University of Chicago Press, 1998), 222.
7. Quoted in Daniel A. Clark, *Creating the College Man: American Mass Magazines and Middle-Class Manhood* (Madison: The University of Wisconsin-Madison, 2010), 3.

"The great enemy of truth is very often not the lie—deliberate, contrived and dishonest—but the myth: persistent, persuasive and unrealistic. Too often we hold fast to the cliches of our forebears. We subject all facts to a prefabricated set of interpretations. We enjoy the comfort of opinion without the discomfort of thought."[1]

John F. Kennedy

10 BAD COMMON ARGUMENTS FOR COLLEGE

by Zak Slayback

Parents, teachers, and guidance counselors happily push bright young people off to four years of college with the belief that it will help them grow into successful, fulfilled adults. "It's the best four years of your life!" "It's so much better than high school!" "It will help you discover yourself and set you on the path to success!"

The praises flow. Parents look forward to the day that they can wear "PROUD MOM OF AN [INSERT UNIVERSITY HERE] STUDENT" t-shirt. Teachers rest on their laurels, tallying how many of their students go to college. Guidance counselors measure their

Zak Slayback is the author of *How to Get Ahead* and a principal at 1517 Fund, a venture capital fund backed by Peter Thiel. He writes at ZakSlayback.com.

school's success by the rate at which it places students at universities.

Most of the time, young people don't question the advice and apply to colleges and universities without giving it much of a second thought. Why should they? The people whom they have spent years either trying to formally please (i.e., teachers and administrators) or informally please (i.e., parents) have made it clear that this is the option that will please them. But sometimes one of these young people raises their voice and questions the convention. In this case, the adults in their lives are pushed to give substantive reasons for why a bright, high-achieving young person should go to college.

These are ten of the most common arguments I've heard adults—many of whom went to college 20-35 years ago—give young people for entering college and why they are bad arguments.

1. College is the ideal place to learn.
2. College is the best place to network.
3. College is the best way to guarantee you get a job.
4. College gives you confidence for the real world.
5. College is a fun social experience.

6. College gives you access to invaluable educational resources like professors and laboratories.
7. College is a prerequisite for many fields.
8. College is the best environment to try different things and "find yourself."
9. College is the thing you've been working towards these past X-number of years.
10. Going to college can only help you, not harm you.

1. COLLEGE IS THE IDEAL PLACE TO LEARN

This argument works with a romanticized idea of the college experience.

Young people, with a hunger for truth and knowledge, will tackle the big questions of different fields with each other, sitting in Socratic-style seminars and lectures, hearing from luminaries in their respective fields! Professors treat their students as explorers for truth and wisdom! Students treat their professors as revered experts in highly specialized knowledge!

Except that's rarely how people treat college. Even at small liberal arts colleges, most students treat their classes as perfunctory, and many professors treat their students as obstacles, not customers because they aren't; their parents or the federal government providing loans are the real customers, and they are several steps removed from the classroom. Students who are looking for an ideal learning culture may find niches where they can engage in real learning. I was fortunate to land a research fellowship at Penn and work closely with a philosopher on several projects, but that kind of intimacy in learning was not the norm, especially at a large university like Penn.

How does this culture arise? If the romanticized view is of people who go actually *wanting* to learn, engage deeply in ideas, and get a well-rounded education, then a culture that doesn't support this environment is likely the consequence of people *going to college for reasons other than learning.*

If you asked the average college-bound young person why they are going to college, the vast majority will tell you "so I can get a job." Very few will tell you it is so they can go learn in the ideal learning environment. And those who will tell you that will likely renege on that answer if you posed the question, "Would you still go to learn and be willing to pay the costs associated with it even if you didn't land a job afterward?"

College doesn't meet the romanticized ideal because it is exactly that: a romanticized ideal. The reality is that it is primarily used as a mechanism for young people to go and increase their chances of landing a high-paying job at age 23. (I tackle this reason below.)

Even further, more and more evidence indicates that the traditional college lecture isn't a good way of teaching people things they want to learn.[2] While people learn in different ways, all people learn best when they are engaged in meaningful behavior that they derive value from. Just as a child is likely to ask "why?" to every assignment, college students give less attention to and glean less information from assignments and activities that they can't meaningfully engage in. Most theory is only really ingrained in people once it has been applied in practice, and only then when that practice is something they derive value from. Even if college was good at meeting its romanticized ideal, the romanticized ideal is only good for teaching certain things. The classroom-based model for education is itself antithetical to meaningful learning.

Some colleges are better at providing an ideal learning environment than others. Great books programs, for example, are particularly good at this and do stay fairly close to the romanticized ideal, but they also tend to be smaller, less-popular programs. Programs at elite research universities like Penn, Michigan, Cornell, Stanford, and others are furthest from the ideal.

Professors are primarily hired to *research*, not to teach. It's no surprise, then, that students leave happier with their education from great books schools than schools like Penn—my own "opted-out mater."

2. COLLEGE IS THE BEST PLACE TO NETWORK

Even Sam Altman, one of the founders of the successful Y Combinator in Silicon Valley, says that college is probably the best place to network.[3] Though he also notes that if you have the opportunity to join a startup with the potential to blow up in the coming years, you should take it and not go to college. Most of the members of the PayPal Mafia—a group of the company's founders and employees who went on to found a number of successful technology companies— went to two or three select schools. Travis Kalanick, the founder of Uber, founded his first company with classmates who dropped out of UCLA with him.

College definitely has potential as a place for ambitious young people to begin networking. Being surrounded by other people looking to achieve something in the world creates an air of importance to each friend, and a lack of major commitments outside of school makes committing to a high-risk project easier.

But this doesn't make college the *best* place to network.

A successful network has to have several components. It must be **horizontally varied** (i.e., containing people in different sectors and industries) and **vertically varied** (i.e., containing people at different stages of life and careers). This allows you to pull on people in a large number of areas as well as those at varying stages of their careers, producing a large number of opportunities from your network.

College networks can be heavily weighted to being horizontally varied, with classmates studying philosophy, engineering, economics, and more, but they tend not to be very vertically varied. Save for a handful of connections made through alumni events, most people in your college network are going to be in essentially the same stage of life as you. They are not going to be the CEOs of successful companies, published authors with several books under their belts, or somebody even 5 or 6 years in advance of you in the startup process.

If you are an entrepreneurial young person who already has an extensive network through extracurricular activities, clubs founded, or other personal connections, you can pour your resources into those to expand them even further, especially since they are likely to atrophy if you go away to college. You probably already do have some vertical and horizontal variance in these networks—don't let them die out for a mediocre college network!

Even further, if you have an opportunity to do something in lieu of college, like a program, fellowship, or a startup project with some outside interest, you already have a framework and the infrastructure necessary to expand the size of your network. Using myself as an example, my network now is infinitely more valuable than the network of some of my peers getting ready to graduate. It contains people at every stage of life in nearly every field of work, and it replenishes itself over time.

College can be a good place to network, but it isn't the best.

3. COLLEGE IS THE BEST WAY TO GUARANTEE YOU WILL GET A JOB

"Well, sure, college seems to be a huge waste of time and resources, but I need it to get *some* kind of job."

There's some logic to this, at least at face value. Employers use college degrees as a way of weeding out certain candidates for jobs. Job candidates use it as a signaling mechanism.[4] If only a handful of people have college degrees, and these degrees indicate that this person is more capable than somebody without it, then it makes sense for employers to look at these.

Except, more often, that's not the case.

In an ideal situation, having a college degree signals to employers that you are a top-notch candidate—somebody who knows how to grind things out and do high-level research, all with a drive that cannot be challenged. In the real world, this isn't really the case. As more and more people get college degrees and more jobs require them, the strength of the signal gets weaker and weaker. Ideally, it signals that you are a bright, enthusiastic young person grasping a diploma after writing a complex thesis and getting four years of the best educational experience possible.

In reality, employers treat a degree as a "minimally viable candidate" signal. To them, the degree from an intelligent young person who strove for success through four years of college means just as much (or as little) as the degree from a guy who showed up hungover to class (when he showed up) and partied four nights a week.

The people who have the most to *lose* by going to college are the people of above-average intelligence or work ethic. Their degree signals the same thing as the person of below-average intelligence or work ethic who goes.

Even if you don't buy all this about the decreasing strength of the signaling power of the degree, just look around at the number of people with college degrees working jobs that don't require degrees for your evidence. There are more janitors with chemistry degrees in the US today than there are chemists.[5]

Meanwhile, jobs that *don't* require college degrees see gains in demand and, therefore, salary. Crane operators can make upwards of $50,000 a year for small operations, and operators in major cities have been reported to make up to $500,000 a year.[6] Marketing agencies are happy to hire candidates without college degrees if they have experience and know how to write good copy. Even major airlines, pushed to ameliorate a coming pilot shortage, are happy to hire candidates without college degrees.[7]

Entrepreneurial young people shouldn't even have to worry about this argument for college, though. They know that whatever comes their way, they'll find a way to pay the bills. Who cares about landing a corporate job that requires a BA to apply when you have 15 ideas for companies you want to launch?

If you do want to pursue this entrepreneurial path, sometimes dropping out or foregoing college altogether can be a more powerful signal than sticking it out.[8]

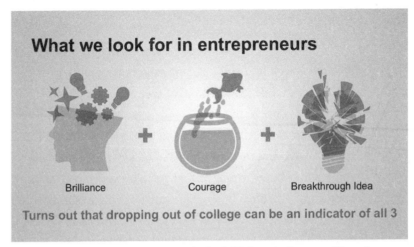

Excerpted from the investment deck of VC firm Andreessen Horowitz.

And honestly, who would want to work for a company that's so stodgy that it wouldn't budge on the BA requirement for an otherwise-well-qualified candidate?

4. COLLEGE GIVES YOU CONFIDENCE FOR THE REAL WORLD

Some people, especially Baby Boomer parents, will attribute their success (and rarely their failure[9]) to the fact that they got a degree from an elite university.

"I wouldn't be where I am today if it wasn't for my time at college!" they may proclaim. Or they say that the challenges and opportunities they had to cope with through college prepared them to go confidently into the real world.

It's entirely possible that working through eight semesters of grueling classes, building camaraderie through Greek life, and just generally putting up with the strife of college may prepare you to approach the real world confidently.

But *actually dealing with the real world* is even more likely to give you the confidence to tackle it. The great thing about being young is that people expect you to screw up, regardless of student status. If you do screw up, no big deal, but you will have more incentives to do better than if you were isolated in the college campus.

Some of the video games I played growing up had "practice" or "arena" levels or other features that allowed me to go around with infinite lives and try different things. Sometimes I would screw up and face a minimal penalty for it. The point of these features was to allow players to try out the game and get a feel for it before playing the game with real stakes.

You spend the first 12 years of your schooling career on practice mode. The sooner you can get into the actual game and try, try, try again, the better. It's going to be hard regardless, so why put it off?

5. COLLEGE IS FUN AND A GREAT SOCIAL EXPERIENCE!

You can hear it now: some dad, drink in hand, chortling, "College was the best four years of my life!"

Imagine the crowds of students at a college football game, playing in the marching band, partying it up at a frat house or with a few friends in the dorm. The sexiness of the college social scene is the subject of hundreds of American comedies.

Here's the thing though: this isn't an argument for college at all. It's an argument for the social scene around it. Most of this can be had without paying four years of your life and tens of thousands of dollars to universities and colleges. You can go to college football games. You can attend college parties. Make friends with a few college students and save yourself the $25,000 that they aren't if you are looking for the college experience.

If you are looking for team spirit and the joys that come with that, just look around yourself at March Madness. The teams people cheer for are rarely their alma maters, but rather the teams *they choose* to like.

If you are looking for a sense of closeness with other people while working towards a common goal, join a program or fellowship for college opt-outs, start your own startup, or join a growing one.

What is also often left unsaid when somebody declares that college was the best four years of their life is that it's because the subsequent years haven't been in their control. The ages people typically attend college are the first time many young people have the freedom to build their own lives. Sometimes they choose to go to college to exert that freedom, and much of the time, older people push them toward that option. They play with this freedom for 3, 4, maybe 5 years, and then set themselves back on a path that puts that freedom on autopilot. They fall into a job that they don't hate, but that they also don't exert their primary control over. They can't feel camaraderie with their coworkers because they don't really choose their coworkers. The people they hang out with and work around just happen to be people who are physically close to them.

By choosing to take control of your education and your life, and maintaining that control, you can also control who you socialize with much more easily. You don't have to worry about 18-22 being the best social years of your life because if a year isn't your best, it's considerably easier for you to make it so.

6. COLLEGE GIVES YOU ACCESS TO INVALUABLE EDUCATIONAL RESOURCES LIKE PROFESSORS AND LABORATORIES

Colleges like to show off the shiny new laboratory they built last year and named after some trustee, or the new floor of the renovated library, or how many professors they have listed with fancy endowed chairs. They like to list these things in their marketing materials because it impresses potential students.

Thankfully, many of the resources that were once concentrated in places like universities are now dispersed across the globe thanks to the Internet. Entire libraries are now available online. Lecture slides from Ivy League universities can be found with a simple Google search. Yale Open Courses, Coursera, and Khan Academy all bring lectures and resources to anybody who has Internet access. Much of the *knowledge* concentrated in universities has been dispersed.

Even still, the idea that college is the only place to access human resources like professors and their colleagues is one that may be true if professors just hid in caves all day, came out to teach and write a little, and went back to their university-owned caves. The reality is that they interact with people in the real world like others do. They attend summer and weekend seminars, write books, have email addresses (and sometimes respond to emails sent to that address!), and can be contacted. Sometimes they contract with independent programs to do guest lectures or exams. They may even appear on the radio or on television to talk about a topic and give out contact information.

The point is that college isn't the only place to access the knowledge of professors. Many professors are flattered to receive emails from enthusiastic young people inquiring about the work they are doing. There are ways to gain access to them if somebody really wants to build a close partnership with a professor.

Capital resources provide another kind of challenge. While knowledge can go anywhere that somebody has an Internet browser, laboratories are much harder to turn into bits and bytes.

Thankfully, university-level laboratories are mostly only useful to those with niche interests in high-level research. As globalization drives the cost of equipment production down, and as more and more universities look to update their equipment, smaller companies are acquiring laboratory equipment that was once out of their reach. Further, with the growth of biotech, start-ups build partnerships with these capital-laden universities to gain access to their resources. So they really aren't entirely off-limits to those outside of universities.

This capital restriction raises a good point about the ease of innovation for somebody lacking heavy resources (like money or political power), though. While anybody with a keyboard and an API can design the next million- or billion-dollar app, it is much harder to invent a new form of steel, or a line of nanobots, or a new drug. The barriers to entry are kept within select institutions like venture-backed startups, universities, and government agencies. If you are looking to innovate in a hard-science field or like a character from *At-*

las Shrugged, you may be best served by looking to find a way into some of these institutions.

7. COLLEGE IS A PREREQUISITE FOR MANY FIELDS

It's no secret that it is impossible (or very, very, very hard) to practice medicine, law, or accounting without an MD, JD, or CPA, respectively. It's hard to tell somebody to completely forego higher schooling if they have a dream of being one of these things.

Similarly, while being an intellectual doesn't require a degree at all,[10] being an academic professor is best served with a Ph.D. (increasingly, so is being a Starbucks barista).

However, this is a very short list of very specific careers.

If you are *very* sure that your life-plan for success must include being in one of these fields, then you will likely have to pursue college first (my advice, then, is to do it as cheaply and quickly as possible with AP credits, dual-enrollments, and merit-based scholarships).

But if your life-plan doesn't include one of these things or working for a massive corporation like Morgan Stanley, then you may be better served by getting experience doing something first. Marketing agencies would happily hire somebody who dropped out of college and spent two years learning marketing copy and digital marketing strategy before they would hire somebody with a marketing degree. Sales can only be learned by joining a sales team, putting together a deck, and building a personal network.

If you want to do any of those things, or the myriad other options that don't require a degree, taking the time, money, and resources to pursue the degree when you *could* be doing something else will actually harm you in the long run. The degree requirement is a barrier-to-entry for some fields but *getting* one can be a barrier-to-entry in others.

8. COLLEGE IS THE BEST ENVIRONMENT TO TRY DIFFERENT THINGS AND "FIND YOURSELF"

If you ask most young people why they are going to college, they will tell you so they can land a job. If you then push them on what job they are looking to land after college, many—even college seniors—won't be able to give you a straight answer. They went to school because they "had to" to get a job (because this is what they'd been told growing up) and they needed to figure out what kind of job they wanted to do.

Turns out that the best way to "find yourself," just like the best way to gain confidence for the real world, is to actually go out into the world and try different things. Even the colleges that offer study abroad programs, consortiums with other universities, and 657 majors and concentrations from 19th Century Analytic Philosophy to Micro-bio-engineering to Underwater Basket Weaving can only offer you so much. A college admissions packet may make it seem like the university offers a varied and interesting experience, but those experiences are still just a very small selection of the experiences available to an 18-year-old American today.

I used to laugh at people who would tell me that they wanted to backpack through Europe or Asia. I still don't think it's necessarily something I would do for myself, but if it is taken as an opportunity to engage meaningfully with the world around you, it can be an infinitely more interesting and enlightening experience than the average four-year college trip.

Here are ten things you can do in four years that are more likely to help you find yourself than dabbling in courses at college. As a bonus, they are probably all cumulatively cheaper than college:

1. Start a blog and commit to contributing to it on a regular basis for a timeframe that you set for yourself.

2. Commit to reading a certain number of books every month.

3. Learn a new language.

4. Travel abroad by yourself for a few months.

5. Learn boating, flying, motorcycling, and the basic maintenance required for each.

6. Learn three new digital skills through local courses, MOOCs, or programs like Codecademy.

7. Learn three new soft skills like public speaking through local groups like Toastmasters.

8. Become certified in a profession, like real estate.

9. Move to a new city.

10. Join a startup team.

All of these things are considerably more likely to lead you to "find yourself," figure out what you like and don't like, and achieve balance in life than drifting through college for four years ever would.

9. COLLEGE IS THE THING YOU'VE BEEN WORKING TOWARDS THESE PAST YEARS

If you've been brought up knowing that others think you are smart, you probably have either crafted much of your schooled life towards building that ideal college application or have had others structure it in this way for you.

For me, high school was a testing ground to see whether I could get into an elite university. I even told my parents, after being admitted to one of my first-choice schools, "This is what I have been working for all these years!" And I hear teachers and parents say the same line to young adults considering foregoing college.

The problem is that this is fallacious thinking.

The idea that you should do something because you have already devoted so many resources to doing so is called the sunk cost fallacy, and it permeates our thinking about college.

Maybe you did devote four or more years of your adolescence to the pursuit of an elite college admission letter. Maybe you gave up nights to study for the ACTs and the SATs. You threw money at extracurricular activities, classes, and programs that you knew would give you the edge you needed to get in. And what? You're going to walk away from all of those resources you used?

Those resources are gone. They aren't coming back. Those nights you spent, those weeks at camp, those dollars on exam prep won't come back if you go to college or if you don't. Don't let yourself fall victim to the sunk cost fallacy.

Just like a person who is in a relationship that is going downhill thinks to themselves, "Well, I spent all that time building this relationship, and all that money on dates, and flowers, and gifts... maybe I should stick with it," it is just as bad an idea to apply the same logic to your career and life-path over the next four years.

Get out now, lest you fall into an abusive relationship with college.

10. GOING TO COLLEGE CAN ONLY HELP YOU, NOT HARM YOU

Admission day comes and you find out that you have been admitted to the elite university that your parents and you (?) have been striving toward. "The world is your oyster! It is my pleasure to have reviewed your application and to admit you to our class!" reads the standard admission letter.

In addition to that, you get a hefty financial aid package that ensures that you won't have to go into debt to complete a degree from this school. You've done it!

But you decide you'd rather not go. You feel that you would rather spend your time learning the things you want to learn with the resources available, launching a few projects, and taking control of your education and your life in a way that you have never known you could before now.

You explain every reason why you don't want to go, and your parents, teachers, and counselors shoot back, "Why not? It can only help you at this point! It won't even cost you a dime!"

This is the key point here. While you are explaining to them all the opportunities you would have if you don't go to school, they forget that included in the cost of attendance isn't just the monetary cost, but also the opportunity cost (the value of the next-best option). Not only could you earn money over these four years, but you could also set yourself on the path to gain experience, develop skills, and launch your own venture while your peers are scurrying to finish midterms.

A FINAL DANGER TO CONSIDER

There is also a very real sense in which continuing schooling immediately after 12 years of schooling *can* harm somebody. People who spend many years and hours being trained to succeed in a very specific system that rewards very specific actions like schools do find themselves having a hard time adapting to the world outside of school. They've come, largely through no fault of their own, to view the world as a series of assignments, tests, due dates, and clear expectations outlined in the student handbook.

This way of viewing the world—what I call "the schooled mind"—only gets worse in college. There is some liberty allowed in choosing and attending classes, but generally speaking, students are still held to assignments, due dates, and other expectations. They fall into a trap of expecting the world to be like this.[11]

Succeeding in an ever-changing world that demands that more people than ever before view themselves as entrepreneurs requires a thorough period of deschooling. Some of the best students at universities can be the worst employees for small organizations. They are too schooled. The person who can deschool themselves early, develop an organic view of the world as a place where value-adds must be identified and created by the individual, not assigned by a manager, will be leaps and bounds ahead of the well-schooled student with a degree from an elite university.

These are just a handful of the bad arguments for going to school, and just a small sample of potential rebuttals to them, that I've encountered in my time of talking to high school students, college students, teachers, counselors, parents, and mentors. At the end of the day, the important thing is for the young person to be able to take control of their life as their own and to be in the driver's seat of their education. Parents can provide useful input, and may have a serious say if they are financing the experience, but young people need to embrace the radical freedom they can seize for themselves at age 18 or 19 and make the most of it. Turn off the autopilot, take control, and go build something great.

NOTES

1. Quoted in Arthur Meier Schlesinger, *A Thousand Days: John F. Kennedy in the White House* (Boston: Houghton Mifflin Company, 1965), 645.
2. "Rethinking the Way College Students Are Taught," American Public Media, accessed May 9, 2019, http://americanradioworks.publicradio.org/features/tomorrows-college/lectures/rethinking-teaching.html.
3. Sam Altman, "Advice for Ambitious 19 Year Olds," SamAltman.com, June 24, 2013, http://blog.samaltman.com/advice-for-ambitious-19-year-olds.
4. Bryan Caplan, "You Might Be Signaling," EconLog, September 18, 2012, http://www.econlib.org/archives/2012/09/you_might_be_si.html.
5. Richard Vedder, "Twelve Inconvenient Truths about American Higher Education," Center for College Affordability and Productivity, March 2012, https://files.eric.ed.gov/fulltext/ED541358.pdf.
6. Joseph De Avila, "Crane Operators Top $500,000 in Pay, Benefits," *The Wall Street Journal*, June 25, 2011, https://www.wsj.com/articles/SB10001424052702303936704576399563008284024.
7. Anthony Balderrama, "25 Highest Paying Jobs -- No Bachelor's Degree Required," AOL, June 26, 2009, https://www.aol.com/2009/06/26/25-highest-paying-jobs-no-bachelors-degree-required/.
8. Henry Blodget, "Here's The Magic Formula For Building Massive Companies," Business Insider, February 1, 2013, https://www.businessinsider.com/how-andreessen-horowitz-chooses-investments-2013-2.
9. Zak Slayback, "Schooling is Not Education, Or, A Lesson in Status Quo Bias," ZakSlayback.com, March 18, 2015, http://zakslayback.com/2015/03/18/schooling-is-not-education-or-a-lesson-in-status-quo-bias/.

10. James Walpole, "The Unschooled Intellectual," Praxis, accessed May 9, 2019, https://discoverpraxis.com/the-unschooled-intellectual/.

11. Zak Slayback, "The College Trap and the Schooled Mind, ZakSlayback.com, accessed May 9, 2019, http://zakslayback.com/2015/03/21/the-college-trap-and-the-schooled-mind/.

"If you don't design your own life plan, chances are you'll fall into someone else's plan. And guess what they have planned for you? Not much."[1]

Jim Rohn

HOW DROPPING OUT OF COLLEGE CAN GIVE YOU A HEAD START ON LIFE

by Derek Magill

The other day I discovered my old University of Michigan student ID card in a stack of papers.

When I saw the future expiration date, a terrifying thought occurred to me: *I could still be in college.*

In other words, I could still be sitting in classes I didn't like and doing things that added no value to my life so I could please administrators, parents, and friends.

I'm twenty-three years old and had I stayed in college, I'd be no better off professionally than I was at 18.

Derek Magill writes, researches, markets and builds businesses in college alternatives, careers, Bitcoin, and freedom. Follow him on Twitter at @DerekMagill.

I know this because many of my peers have graduated recently, and they're finding the only options available to them are unpaid or low paying internships.

I want to tell you some of what I did over these last three or so years instead of being in school. Dropping out of college has given me a huge head start, and it can do the same for you if you use the time wisely.

Keep in mind that I'm nowhere near as productive as I'd like to be. I procrastinate, miss opportunities, burn bridges, and fail to deliver on many of my goals. As I hope to show you, you don't need to be operating at 100% all the time in the real world to accomplish many things.

THE REAL WORLD VS. THE SCHOOLED WORLD

If there is one thing I've realized, it's that the real world moves much faster than the schooled world. In the absence of hoop jumping, bureaucratic roadblocks, and arbitrary standards, the pace of your life can dramatically accelerate.

After four years of school, I would have graduated with some friends, a few essays that nobody would ever read, and a piece of paper that said "degree" on it.

Within a few months of time in the real world, I'd made more friends than I ever made in college, written dozens of blog posts, and started getting work opportunities despite not having a credential.

I've seen people do even more than that.

In my work at Praxis, I've had people leave college and write a book within three or four months. I've seen people launch podcasts. Some of them have traveled more than most people do in their lifetimes. Others have been promoted into positions at companies that people with five years of experience couldn't get.

In contrast, many of my friends from high school have not accomplished anything since getting accepted into college. They're graduating with very little to show for the last four years.

The period between ages 18-25 can either be some of the most important, most productive periods of your life or they can be a washout.

This is why I always tell kids that it's pretty much risk free to take time off from college. Things move so slowly in school that the potential downside is small, while the potential upside of trying something on your own can be massive.

WHAT I DID INSTEAD OF ATTENDING COLLEGE

The first thing to know is that I had almost no plan when I dropped out. Although dropouts like Ryan Holiday say you should have something lined up before you leave college, I think that's wrong for a number of reasons:

1. Most college students have no idea what they want to do or what the world really offers. You can't discover this in college, so waiting for the "perfect" opportunity is a fool's task.

2. Your goals will change rapidly once you leave school. Since you have very little experience, the first opportunity you pursue might be a total bust. You might realize you hate it. You probably will. What then?

In most cases, you must remove yourself from school to start seeing things the way they are. There's never a "right time" to take the red pill. You just have to make the leap and hope for the best.

Since I had no clear path, I decided to start trying a ton of things:

*   I did some work for my parent's company and built an eBay and an Amazon store. I taught myself how to do this in a few days with Google.
*   I offered to work for free for a family friend and landed him as a client.

- I bought a camera and started taking photos at events. Some of the organizers liked my work and purchased it.

- I used that camera to start filming videos as well and shot for a few local businesses in San Diego.

- I ran Instagram and Facebook accounts for my family's business and several other companies.

- I did graphic design for Colliers International, a commercial real estate company.

- I drove around Texas taking photos of restaurants for real estate companies.

- I took a job in Austin at a media company called Vici Media Group.

- I started making standing desks from parts purchased at IKEA and selling them on eBay with my friend, Glenn.

- I began blogging a bit.

- I negotiated a $300,000 multiyear software deal with Netsuite.

Somewhere during that process, I started to zero in on what I was good at and what I wanted to do with my time.

My marketing client base began to grow and soon I was making good money. In fact, I was making great money. A Facebook ad I ran for a client blew up and paid my dividends for the entirety of 2015. I registered a business that was informally called Maggle Social.

The first eight months or so out of school were some of the most enlightening times of my life.

I realized, for example, that most professionals weren't as knowledgeable as they seemed. I learned that you can learn much more quickly by imitation than by reading or studying. I saw that businesses don't really care about degrees and I discovered how to get them to work with you even if you didn't have a degree or formal experience. I began learning personal finance and health habits, and I started to see more clearly the kind of life I wanted to have.

Many of the material goals I had in college fell away as I began to take more and more pleasure in the process of working and producing something that others found valuable.

These are things I could have never learned in school.

During this time, I was also attending conferences and reading on my own. I found my love of learning came back quickly when I wasn't spending my time following somebody else's syllabus and studying things that didn't interest me.

Classics. Economics. Philosophy. Self-Improvement. Business.

These were all topics I explored, and I read more during that time than almost any time in my life.

The next two years got even better.

Praxis became a client of mine. I worked with them for a year, traveled all around the country, was interviewed by dozens of podcasts, developed my writing skills, and learned marketing through doing marketing in a way I never got to through contract work. I saw the ins and outs of running a small but growing startup and I got in on the ground floor of something I think is going to be huge. I soon became their Director of Marketing.

It takes years for most people to become a head of marketing, but the opportunity presented itself because I'd spent the previous year or so creating opportunities that led to other opportunities and so on.

I started getting speaking opportunities and have now spoken at universities around the country, as well as in Austin, San Diego, Salt Lake City, and Washington, D.C. I've even spoken to groups in Serbia and Bosnia. In fact, I'm writing this while I'm on a plane headed to Prague where I'll be speaking at Charles University.

Being involved with Praxis taught me a ton about business and gave me a level of credibility I would not have had on my own. I started getting bigger and better opportunities and now I have to actively turn things away.

Over the past year, I've traveled more than 130,000 miles and visited a dozen countries. This all cost less than a semester of college tuition and I didn't travel cheaply. I know people who are graduating now who want to travel but can't because of all the debt they have. They could have worked a part-time job during a gap year and traveled as much or more than I did.

I also put together an eBook called *How to Get Any Job You Want* that has been downloaded thousands of times and helped kids all over the world get jobs that would otherwise be closed to them.

In the past nine months, Praxis has more than quadrupled in size. Instead of taking classes, I spent my recent "fall semester" overseeing the buildout of a new customer relationship marketing system and traveling through Greece and Eastern Europe.

My writings, videos, and Quora posts have over a million views total and I get messages every day from people from Ecuador to India asking how they can leave college, too.

Setting aside all of the above, the most valuable thing I've gained from this time out of school is self-knowledge. I never could have imagined I'd be doing what I do now for a career. Teachers, parents, and experienced professionals all told me to pursue a narrow set of cookie cutter careers like law, medicine, or finance.

The idea that I could be traveling, writing, building a startup that is redefining higher education, and running a business of my own—all by the age of twenty-three—was something that was never on my radar.

I know more clearly what I want out of the next few years of my life, and I don't stress about the uncertainty beyond that. I trust that knowledge will come with time and experience.

Compare this all to school and class time. What could I have gained by staying there for three more years?

WHAT I WISH I'D KNOWN

I get emails all the time from kids who want to drop out, but they see some of what I'm working on and doubt that they will have the same success.

The truth that it took me a long time to realize is that the bar is quite low, and you usually don't need more education to get started. Most of what I listed above could have been accomplished faster if I'd just acted and put something out into the world rather than trying to make sure everything was perfect.

The more I adopted a mindset of "just build it and ship it" the more I started to see actual returns.

If you're in the same shoes I was a few years ago, don't worry. Start now and try tons of things. You'll be surprised how much will come your way.

I also wish I had learned earlier how to pursue new opportunities.

But you don't have to go through the hassle that I did.[2] Most job requirements can be totally sidestepped using a number of simple tactics. It's so easy you'll laugh that you didn't see it before.

NOTES

1. Quoted in John C. Maxwell, *Developing the Leader Within You 2.0* (Nashville: HarperCollins, 2018), 216.
2. Derek Magill, "How to Get a Job Even if You Don't Have a College Degree," DerekMagill.com, https://derekmagill.com/2016/06/15/how-to-get-any-job-you-want/.

"The only way to do great work is to love what you do. If you haven't found it yet, keep looking. Don't settle."[1]

Steve Jobs

LEARN WHAT YOU LOVE

by Connor Boyack

Having written over a dozen books, people often assume that I studied in school what I now write and teach about: politics, history, economics, and education. I chuckle at this assumption because it's not just false, it completely contradicts my reality.

A few years ago, my mother ran into one of my high school English teachers. My mother informed this teacher—who remembered me well, which is probably a bad thing—that I was now an accomplished author and writing prolifically as part of my full-time profession as the head of a political think tank, Libertas Insti-

---

Connor Boyack is president of Libertas Institute, a free market think tank in Utah. He is author of over a dozen books, including the acclaimed children's book series The Tuttle Twins. Learn more at ConnorBoyack.com.

tute. The teacher was astounded to learn this because I had been anything but a star student in her class.

Here's the thing: I *hated* English class. Economics and history were similarly loathsome to me, and I didn't enjoy or perform well in any of these subjects during high school or college. So, perhaps you can see why my English teacher would be surprised to hear a young man had transitioned from writing unintelligible, awkwardly constructed essays to writing an array of books that other people are actually willing to pay to read and that I've sold well over half a million of them.

The pertinent question is: how did this happen? How did I come to love and excel in the very subjects that I detested during my school years? How is it that I came to love learning about the things that once turned me off? How did I build a successful career out of it?

The answer: *freedom.*

Don't write this answer off as trite or simplistic, because there are substantial and compelling reasons to base our educational approach upon the philosophy of freedom and plenty of practical ways to apply it to every subject under the sun.

I went to college. I didn't know any different; my parents didn't expose me to any alternatives nor was I made aware of them, as you have been with this book. And when I graduated, I was finally free from all of the exams, projects, and homework that were more of a hindrance than a help toward achieving my goals. I was no longer required to "learn" facts and figures that had no apparent relevance or interest to me, only to regurgitate them for a grade and, inevitably, to forget them soon after. Once I obtained my degree, I had more free time than ever before and the ability to focus my time and mental energy on things which mattered to me. Finally, I had freedom.

So, I read—slowly at first. After so many years of studying what others had chosen on my behalf, my curiosity muscles had atrophied. I soon found that as I read the books I wanted, my curiosity began to grow, and so, I read some more. I began to write about what I was learning and gained a growing readership. That audience made me keenly aware of how awful I was at writing; reviewing what I wrote back then is painful for me now. But my embarrassment became an internal motivation to improve. I now had a compelling reason to learn how to write well.

To do so, I didn't crack open my English textbook from college. (Actually, like most students, I sold that ten-pound paperweight as soon as I could.) I didn't begin a technical review of the semantic structure of persuasive writing, fretting over compound pluperfect subjunctives and other mind-numbing minutiae.

Instead, I observed and imitated. I read material from authors who wrote well, and I made their practices my own until it became natural for me to communicate well, too. I learned by doing, guided by those who were masters of their craft.

Today, my interests and expertise are in the very subjects which I suffered through in school. It was the freedom to pursue these areas of study on my own terms that inspired me to actively pursue the information I had previously deemed to be useless and dull. This freedom to seek knowledge, once I fully grasped its relevance, opened a new world to me—one that has turned into a fulfilling career allowing me to influence the lives of tens of thousands of other people.

I offer the foregoing information about myself to explain why I believe so passionately that freedom to pursue your individual interests is the most effective way to help you become educated adults because—let's be honest—all lasting education is self-motivated. We cannot compel a person to learn anything. People who are forced to learn undesired information will allow it to slip from their memory, if they ever learned it at all. As the saying goes, "A man convinced against his will is of the same opinion still." College just perpetuates this problem.

I believe the most effective and natural form of education is one that centers on the interests of the individual. Once you develop a passion—even if you later find new ones—learning will transition from a chore to a joy. Finding purpose and meaning in what we learn makes education lose all of the drudgery, compulsion, and stress that too many adults dismiss as the acceptable collateral damage of the learning process. It doesn't have to be that way.

SO... WHAT'S THE PROBLEM?

Each of us is, by nature, a curious creature. A baby's brain development is astonishingly accelerated; from the moment of conception, the neurons in a baby's brain multiply faster than any other type of cell. By age three, a child's brain has developed so quickly that it has already grown to 90% of its final adult weight. Constantly observing their surroundings, and imitating what they see as best they can, babies are inherently enthralled by the world around them. Every new stimulus is an opportunity to explore and learn.

Now, think of many of your peers—the average teenager. Often, they are apathetic, uninvolved, disinterested, and complaining about overwhelming amounts of homework that encroaches upon their limited free time. For too many, their natural desire to learn has been turned into a chore that breeds resentment and disdain. How can this outcome be explained? Why do so many children go from absorbing information to becoming resistant to it? More importantly, how can we learn from and avoid this trend for ourselves?

The first thing we need to do is recognize that *education does not equate to school.* The former is not bound by buildings, schedules, and formalized instruction. Too many people have so conflated the two in their minds, and many children are being raised to perceive their free time and personal interests as separate from and unrelated to their education. If we don't realize that education happens outside of structured schooling, then is it any wonder society pushes young adults to spend years more inside a college classroom?

One of the things I remember most about school was looking at the clock, counting down the minutes until class time was over. The segmentation of education—treating it as something to be scheduled and structured—conditions children to see learning as a chore. The system teaches them that if they suffer a little longer, they will earn a few minutes to visit with friends, grab a snack, or listen to some music. The psychological effects of this are unavoidable: by withholding freedom until class is over or an assignment is complete, children come to feel that learning is a hindrance to what they really want to do.

Most of us have been subjected in school to coercive methods of education, as described above. We were told *what* to study, *when*, and, in most cases, *where*. When we asked *why*, our teacher may have replied, "You have to," or "It's the law," while a parent might say, "Because I said so," or the rarely true "Because someday you'll need to know it."

Coercion—the opposite of freedom—is the root of many of the problems of modern education. But by no means is it the only one; the schooling system, of which college plays an integral part, is chock full of them.

CRAMMING INFORMATION

Ben Orlin is a high school math teacher in Oakland, California. When he addressed the assembled students in his first-ever trigonometry class, he asked them what the sine of $\pi/2$ is. Their unified answer, "One!" indicated that they had already covered the material. "We learned that last year," they told their teacher.

Like any new teacher, Orlin zipped ahead through the material, but came to realize that the students didn't really know what "sine" actually meant—they had merely memorized the answer to the question. "To them," Orlin writes, "math wasn't a process of logical discovery and thoughtful exploration. It was a call-and-response game. Trigonometry was just a collection of non-rhyming lyrics to the lamest sing-along ever."

Imagine yourself as this math teacher trying to teach trigonometry. Chances are, you're going to rely upon a textbook or some other form of curriculum to do the teaching for you. Your student will be expected to absorb the information presented in the book, and so, he or she packs away that tidbit in the back of his or her brain: the sine of $\pi/2$ is one. However, as Orlin notes, this information-heavy approach to education is not ideal:

> Some things are worth memorizing—addresses, PINs, your parents' birthdays. The sine of $\pi/2$ is not among them. It's a fact that matters only insofar as it connects to other ideas. To learn it in isolation is like learning the sentence "Hamlet kills Claudius" without the faintest idea of who either gentleman is—or, for that matter, of what "kill" means. Memorization is a frontage road: It runs parallel to the best parts of learning, never intersecting. It's a detour around all the action, a way of knowing without learning, of answering without understanding.

Regurgitation of information gives the appearance of knowledge mastery while masking the reality of poor comprehension. I did this all the time in school—and I'm betting you have as well. It's a way for a person to falsely demonstrate retention without having to achieve comprehension.

Part of the school experience is *cramming*—spending hours before an exam pushing as much information as possible into our brains, in the hopes that one of the factoids happens to be what the teacher wants to quiz us on. Sometimes you were allowed to use notes or a small "cheat sheet," leading to minuscule text being packed into the limited space so as to maximize one's chance of success.

Is that education? Is it how you want to explore the world and acquire knowledge? Is it healthy? Is it effective? These are some of the most basic questions we can ask, yet if we ask them sincerely, the answers are plainly obvious. Why, then, do we do it? Peter Kaufman, a professor of sociology at the State University of New York, observed:

> As a college professor, I see the dysfunctional effects of an educational system based on testing when I look out into a room full of students. After years of cramming, memorizing, regurgitating, and forgetting, many students enter college with little intellectual curiosity, much less a sense of academic excitement. Too often, the students just want to be told what they need to learn to pass the test or what they need to write to get a good grade on a paper. Because so much

of their schooling has been based on this dys-
functional model, they have forgotten how to
be the self-directed and genuine learners that
they were when they first entered school.

I recently came across an online forum where
young readers were asked about the most frustrating
part of high school. Reading the responses was both
depressing and a damning indictment of a school system that has a detrimental impact on education. Those
commenting shared horror stories, concerns, and
missed opportunities—a tapestry of disappointment
and conflict.

Unfortunately, this isn't a problem confined to the
United States. Consider this post from Rin Shimizu, a
student in Malaysia, discussing a recent experience in
her chemistry class:

> Teacher: We're gonna learn about Gibbs Free
> Energy today. All you need to know is this little
> symbol, yes, this one here. If there is a negative
> sign in front of the symbol, then a reaction is
> spontaneous. If there is a positive sign, the reac-
> tion is not spontaneous.
>
> **Me:** Why? Why's that?

Teacher: It's just the way it is. That's all you need to know.

Me: Surely there is some reason behind that? I've heard that whether a reaction is spontaneous is related to the enthalpy of a reaction...

Teacher: That's true, but all you need to know is that if there is a negative sign...

This is basically what happens in most of my classes. Questions inquiring beyond the syllabus? Slapped down! Classes are to prepare us for exams and to ace the syllabus, not to acquire knowledge for the sake of learning.

Under this broken model of education, we are taught what to think—as if there exists a base set of core knowledge that every single person needs to learn to be successful in life. We are provided with dates, names, events, processes, equations, and other information to be memorized and regurgitated—but rarely actually used. Reason and inquiry are unnecessary in a system where teachers provide information and then quiz students based on whether they remember it and not whether they actually understand it.

This is a problem—and it happens every day on college campuses.

CLINGING TO STRUCTURE

I remember owning one of those daily calendars where each day presented a different comic. Mine featured the dry-humored *Far Side* series. In one comic, a student with a small head interrupted the class to ask his teacher, "May I be excused? My brain is full." It may be humorous to suggest that information overload is a possibility, but reality tells a different story. Unlike a child's belly or bladder, the brain has an effectively limitless storage capacity. Nearly a billion neurons, each of which connects to nearly 1,000 other neurons, produce a seemingly inexhaustible web of opportunity to store memories. Brains are marvelous creations!

So, the issue isn't information overload per se; we don't need to worry about being subjected to too many facts and figures. The question is one of *organization* and *relevance*.

From our first days as children, we are on a mission to make sense of the world around us. Young children constantly observe their surroundings, process what they see, and try to identify patterns that might predict future behavior. My children understand that when I pick up one of their books, I'm going to ask if I can read to them. If I open a bag of their favorite fruit, I'm going to offer them some. If I buckle my seat belt, I'm going to immediately ask if they've buckled theirs. Each task or technique they're taught—whether through observation and imitation or communication from a parent, peer, or sibling—has direct applicability to their lives. It makes sense, has context, and empowers them.

This process of natural learning is discarded in the modern education system and replaced with an arbitrary one. Parents and teachers often call it "structure." I call it the slow death of curiosity.

Colleges, like modern schools for children, are extremely regimented, both in logistics and learning. Rigorous schedules shuffle us from one classroom to the next lunch. Teachers are given a specific amount of time to teach each group of students, and when the bell rings, the learning must immediately be stopped so that the student can go to the next class. What message does this fragmentation convey?

I'm so excited that John Taylor Gatto contributed a chapter for this book—sadly, it was the last thing he wrote before he passed away. He is an educational hero to many, myself included. Gatto was a teacher for nearly three decades in New York and was named New York State Teacher of the Year in 1991—the same year he quit teaching after penning an op-ed in the Wall Street Journal explaining that he was no longer willing "to hurt kids." His time in the trenches led him to become an outspoken critic of what he called "prime training for permanent underclasses"—a dumbing down of the general population. Of the highly structured schedules found in modern education, Gatto writes:

> But when the bell rings I insist [my students] drop whatever it is we have been doing and proceed quickly to the next work station. They must turn on and off like a light switch. Nothing important is ever finished in my class or in any class I know of. Students never have a complete experience except on the installment plan.

> Indeed, the lesson of bells is that no work is worth finishing, so why care too deeply about anything? Years of bells will condition all but the strongest to a world that can no longer offer important work to do. Bells are the secret logic of school time; their logic is inexorable. Bells destroy the past and future, rendering every interval the same as any other, as the abstraction of a map renders every living mountain and river the same, even though they are not. Bells inoculate each undertaking with indifference.

Time is structured in school, but the content itself is even more packaged and processed before being presented to students. Curriculum committees, textbook developers, school boards, and other faceless groups of people whose motives and goals we do not know—and perhaps do not share—conspire to create lesson plans and curriculum standards that become the narrow tunnel through which we all must pass. There are no detours available, and pausing is out of the question; students are compelled to continue crawling through the tunnel at whatever speed their masters decide. This conveyor belt in our public schools is equally evident in our colleges.

These and other structural problems don't account for your specific strengths and weaknesses or your personal educational goals and interests. They don't tolerate customization based on a student's interests and desires. Studying things outside the mandated structure is acceptable during our free time, but that's unlikely to happen; free time is assaulted by assignments from the teacher.

One-size-fits-all structures treat us as commodities—homogenous products to be impressed upon by the same process and system. Little if any consideration is given to the student's interests, abilities, talents, or goals. Completion of assigned tasks and getting through the material is the primary goal.

But the simple truth is that you're not a cog in a machine; you shouldn't be treated as a dehumanized lemming being led about by people who do not have your best interests at heart. You're a unique person, with talents and interests that should not be suppressed or sidelined in order to follow an educational path that somebody else deems best. Structure is often seen by parents and professional educators as a means to an end, but it has become an end unto itself.

By imposing strict guidelines and requiring the memorization of useless information and the completion of arbitrary tasks, we undermine the very reason the structure supposedly exists in the first place: to introduce students to new ideas and inspire them to seek understanding. Textbooks, workbooks, syllabi, and standardized exams bury students in often meaningless and context-less busywork that on the surface appears to convey knowledge, but more often breeds resentment, frustration, and increasing intolerance towards the very information they otherwise might be thrilled to learn.

This, too, is a problem.

AUTHORITARIANISM

A popular, though fake, image continues to spread through social media depicting a teacher's letter informing a mother that her insubordinate child Alex was sentenced to detention. What did this fictional Alex do that was wrong? "He consistently defied me," wrote the pretend teacher. "During class, he contradicted me numerous times when I insisted that the length of one kilometer was greater than that of one mile."

It gets more interesting. The letter continued: "Although he was correct, Alex's actions show a blatant disregard for authority, and a complete lack of respect for his school. In the future, Alex would be better off simply accepting my teachings without resistance." While it was not a real letter, online forums are filled with people from all grade levels, including college, posting their own similar—and real—experiences facing authoritarian teachers.

This tradition of placing more emphasis on authority than actual truth is troubling. College professors should be facilitators of students acquiring knowledge. Unfortunately, too often, they are perceived to be the source. It gets worse when that supposed source is distanced and abstracted, when central planners who lack a connection to or interest in the needs of individual students produce the information that we are required to learn. These planners may come in the form of bureaucrats and curriculum committees who dictate standards or textbook manufacturers who create books to teach those standards. Are these individuals vetted? How can we identify their biases and philosophies? Why should we take them at their word and treat their statements as unquestionable facts?

While many people in the modern education system are authoritarian, so, too, is the process itself. This
top-down approach to centrally planning the education
of the entire rising generation demonstrates, to quote a
college professor, "the desire to engineer the learning
experiences of every child." There are many education
problems to solve, the professor acknowledges, "but
one-size-fits-all modeling, accompanied by the seemingly limitless urge to repackage and sell old ideas as
new ones" produces a constant stream of "education
reforms" from government at all levels. He continues:

> States adopt untested teacher evaluation frame-
> works whole-hog, and the federal government
> attaches new strings to desperately needed fed-
> eral funding without investigating the effective-
> ness of its preferred approaches first. In each
> case, the solution comes before the problem is
> properly defined, and it comes with a dictum
> that cannot be ignored. This is the solution,
> we're told. Now go implement it.

Education should be about inquiry and investiga-
tion—an open-minded review of information as it is discovered and dissected. Ideas should rise and fall on their
merits, and we should constantly be adapting and pro-
gressing, ever trying to find the best ways to do things.
But this cannot happen when you have the few deciding

for the many. Unaccountable and fallible "deciders" who plan the educational roadmap of our lives end up making completely arbitrary decisions about what information we should be exposed to and tested on.

The reality of world history cannot be ignored, and the widespread (and catastrophic) effects of authoritarian education methodologies must be heeded by everyone. Conditioning children and young adults to look to their teacher or textbook as the source of unquestionable truth breeds an unhealthy dependence that will be difficult to overcome as an adult. It also sets you up to become controlled by others. If you are accustomed to life on a factory conveyor belt, then you are subject to the whim and will of whoever controls the machine—and a conveyor belt that mass produces subservient citizens is a very enticing system that tempts a wide range of people, from well-intentioned (though misguided) education reformers to power-hungry utopian tyrants hoping to shape society into their ideal image.

And this is a problem.

WHAT ARE YOUR GOALS?

On June 25, 2010, 18-year-old Erica Goldson stood at a podium in front of her peers and their parents.

Behind her sat the administrators and teachers of the school from which she was graduating. As school valedictorian, Erica now had the opportunity to speak to her graduating class.

To say that Erica's words were unexpected would be a tremendous understatement. The speech was akin to dropping a grenade into a foxhole filled with both wounded warriors and war generals. It rebuked the very institution in which she excelled and condemned the life work of the salaried school staff who supported her. But where many took offense, others received inspiration from the accurate and honest assessment of the problems through which Erica and her peers had navigated.

"I cannot say that I am any more intelligent than my peers," Erica said. "I can attest that I am only the best at doing what I am told and working the system." She continued:

> Yet, here I stand, and I am supposed to be proud that I have completed this period of indoctrination. I will leave in the fall to go on to the next phase expected of me, in order to receive a paper document that certifies that I am capable of work. But I contest that I am a human being, a thinker, an adventurer—not a worker. A worker is someone who is trapped within repetition—a slave of the system set up before him. But now,

I have successfully shown that I was the best slave. I did what I was told to the extreme.

Ouch.

If the modern education system is a conveyor belt of manufactured learning, then Erica was the Grade A product—the very best commodity the system had produced. She was superior to the rest, jumping through every hoop and following the system's guidelines to the letter. But at what cost? Erica explains:

> While others sat in class and doodled to later become great artists, I sat in class to take notes and become a great test-taker.

> While others would come to class without their homework done because they were reading about an interest of theirs, I never missed an assignment.

> While others were creating music and writing lyrics, I decided to do extra credit, even though I never needed it.

> So, I wonder, why did I even want this position? Sure, I earned it, but what will come of it? When I leave educational institutionalism, will I be successful or forever lost? I have no clue about what I want to do with my life; I have no

interests because I saw every subject of study as work, and I excelled at every subject just for the purpose of excelling, not learning. And quite frankly, now I'm scared.

If a model student like Erica is terrified of her future, and ill-equipped to face it, then what is the point of the system at all? The quality of output compels us to question the process used to create it.

Think about yourself—do you want to be a good test-taker and instruction follower? Or, perhaps, we should strive to be something more than a human equivalent of Pavlov's dog?

My goals and desires can't be assessed by a test or learned in a workbook. I want to develop a vibrant personality and qualities such as courage, leadership, creativity, empathy, persistence, innovation, resilience, motivation, etc. I want to be constantly curious and eager to use my talents in the service of others. These, and a host of other positive traits, are what any parent wants for their children. But can we rely on colleges to cultivate them? The answer is clear.

More than anything, you should want to be prepared for the future—equipped with the tools and training necessary to navigate your way through uncharted territory. That preparation won't come by regurgitation or standardized examination. College doesn't necessarily provide you with what you need. A different process—a different path—is needed. And as you've seen in this book, there are many such paths available to you.

Part of the challenge is that your path in life is not linear and safely guarded by padded rails on either side. Given the unpredictability of the future, it's better to visualize your life as having many forks in the road and presenting choices and the corresponding consequences, depending on which direction you choose to travel. Rapid changes in technology are making many professions obsolete and creating entirely new ones; attending school to learn a skill is no guarantee that that skill will be in demand for years to come. Consider today's managers of e-commerce companies, many of whom went to college before the industry even existed. It's better to anticipate uncertainty and develop skills that have general application—leadership, ingenuity, curiosity, persistence, etc.—than to put all your educational eggs in one career basket. You want to be successful no matter how the economy changes or what circumstances they face as they go through life.

A few months after the valedictorian speech, Erica was asked to suggest three pieces of advice she would give to high school students who face an unpredictable world. She offered the following:

1. Don't take school too seriously. Sometimes that picture you're drawing is more important than studying for your Spanish test.

2. Get involved. Find your passions and explore them even more by joining or forming clubs.

3. Meet a lot of people. Learn as much as you can about what other people think and how little you actually know.

You'll notice that she didn't emphasize getting good grades, doing all your homework, or making sure to thoroughly complete the curriculum. Instead, her sound advice, if implemented, will lead you to new experiences, new relationships, new perspectives, and an enriched sense of community and personal character—all things that your parents desire in a well-rounded child primed for success in life. After all, the best lessons in life are often not found in a book.

CRITICAL THINKING

Perhaps one of the most important goals we should establish—and one of the characteristics that many colleges utterly fail to cultivate—is that of critical thinking: the ability to objectively evaluate an issue to form a judgment. Put differently, critical thinking involves questioning proposed information, formulating arguments for or against it, and making decisions based on presented evidence.

Critical thinking is inherently anti-authoritarian. Those who have this capacity do not accept information merely because of its source. "Because I said so" isn't good enough; ideas must rise and fall based on the message, rather than the messenger.

Many in the "mainstream" educational establishment struggle with these approaches, because critical thinking is difficult to quantify, and therefore difficult to assess. In other words, school administrators can't sit you down, give you a fill-in-the-bubble exam, and compute a score to see if you developed this trait.

These assessment-driven, authority-based school systems of the past century are a recent development in human history, whereas student-centric approaches have long existed. For example, the Socratic method— where learners are engaged in an analytic discussion, rather than a passive presentation—is over 2,400 years old. Reformers like to be "new" and "fresh," with ever-changing criteria of "best practices," but the results of lecture-based learning (a staple on college campuses) are consistently poor. For example, a 2005 study showed that only fifteen percent of high school seniors who were already deemed "proficient" in writing were actually able to write well-organized essays in which they took clear positions and consistently supported those positions with evidence. Even worse, only six percent of them could make informed, critical judgments about written text they were asked to read.

The risk is clear: those who cannot formulate coherent arguments and analyze supporting statements are susceptible to believing falsehoods. An ignorant society is a gullible society, easily led down dangerous paths based on misinformation, propaganda, and fear of the unknown. Critical thinking, on the other hand, empowers you to discern facts from spin and arrive at conclusions and decisions that are evidenced-based and supportable by reason and objective data.

But we must be cautious, because critical thinking is a term that has been co-opted, much like a snake oil salesman's use of the word "cure" to describe his worthless product. The simple fact that the term has been increasingly bandied about does not mean that more people are actually developing the skills and techniques that equate to critical thinking. As of 2014, "mentions of critical thinking in job postings ha[d] doubled since 2009," according to the *Wall Street Journal*. Their analysis found that "more than 21,000 health-care and 6,700 management postings contained